This book should be returned to any branch of the
Lancashire County Library on or before the date

PEARSON

At Pearson, we believe in learning – all kinds of learning for all kinds of people. Whether it's at home, in the classroom or in the workplace, learning is the key to improving our life chances.

That's why we're working with leading authors to bring you the latest thinking and best practices, so you can get better at the things that are important to you. You can learn on the page or on the move, and with content that's always crafted to help you understand quickly and apply what you've learned.

If you want to upgrade your personal skills or accelerate your career, become a more effective leader or more powerful communicator, discover new opportunities or simply find more inspiration, we can help you make progress in your work and life.

Pearson is the world's leading learning company. Our portfolio includes the Financial Times and our education business, Pearson International.

Every day our work helps learning flourish, and wherever learning flourishes, so do people.

To learn more, please visit us at **www.pearson.com/uk**

The Financial Times

With a worldwide network of highly respected journalists, *The Financial Times* provides global business news, insightful opinion and expert analysis of business, finance and politics. With over 500 journalists reporting from 50 countries worldwide, our in-depth coverage of international news is objectively reported and analysed from an independent, global perspective.

To find out more, visit **www.ft.com/pearsonoffer/**

25 need-to-know management models

Gerben van den Berg
Paul Pietersma

PEARSON

Harlow, England • London • New York • Boston • San Francisco • Toronto • Sydney
Auckland • Singapore • Hong Kong • Tokyo • Seoul • Taipei • New Delhi
Cape Town • São Paulo • Mexico City • Madrid • Amsterdam • Munich • Paris • Milan

Pearson Education Limited
Edinburgh Gate
Harlow CM20 2JE
United Kingdom
Tel: +44 (0)1279 623623
Web: www.pearson.com/uk

First published 2015 (print and ele[

© Berenschot BV 2015 (print and e[

Pearson Education is not responsible for the content of third-party internet sites.

ISBN: 978-1-292-01635-1 (print)
978-1-292-01637-5 (PDF)
978-1-292-01638-2 (ePub)
978-1-292-01636-8 (eText)

British Library Cataloguing-in-Publication Data
A catalogue record for the print edition is available from the British Library

Library of Congress Cataloging-in-Publication Data
Berg, Gerben van den.
  25 need-to-know management models / Gerben van den Berg, Paul Pietersma.
    pages cm
  Includes bibliographical references and index.
  ISBN 978-1-292-01635-1 (limp : alk. paper)
    1. Organizational effectiveness. I. Pietersma, Paul. II. Title. III. Title: Twenty-five
  need-to-know management models.
  HD31.B3953 2015
  658--dc23
                        2014035230

10 9 8 7 6 5 4 3 2 1
18 17 16 15 14

Cover design by Two Associates

Print edition typeset in 9pt StoneSerif by 30
Print edition printed in Great Britain by Henry Ling Ltd, at the Dorset Press, Dorchester, Dorset

NOTE THAT ANY PAGE CROSS REFERENCES REFER TO THE PRINT EDITION

Contents

About the authors

Gerben van den Berg (MScBA) is a senior strategy consultant at Berenschot in the Netherlands. He has advised clients in a range of industries across Europe. In his consulting practice, his core area of work is in strategy development, competitive positioning, corporate governance and complex organisational transformation. Gerben has a special interest in professional service firms. He is the author of numerous books and articles on strategy and management that have been translated into more than ten languages, including the bestselling *Key Management Models* (Pearson, 2014) and the internationally well-received *The 8 Steps to Strategic Success*.

Paul Pietersma (MScBA MMC) is a strategy consultant and managing director of strategy, funding and innovation at Berenschot in the Netherlands. He has over 15 years' experience in the consulting business, during which time he has advised many CEOs and boards of directors in a wide range of industries in the Netherlands, Belgium, Africa and the Caribbean. He has won the Dutch Professionals Award for Management Consultancy. He is the author of numerous books and articles on strategy and management, including the bestselling previous edition of *Key Management Models* (Pearson, 2014), the internationally well-received *The 8 Steps to Strategic Success* and several leading titles in Dutch.

Publisher's acknowledgements

This book is based on content from *Key Management Models*, first written by Steven ten Have and Wouter ten Have, alongside contributions from Frans Stevens, and developed for the second edition by Marcel van Assen, Paul Pietersma and Gerben van den Berg, and for the third edition by Gerben van den Berg and Paul Pietersma.

We are grateful to the following for permission to reproduce copyright material:

Figures 1.1 and 1.2 after *Corporate Strategy*, revised edition, Penguin Books (Ansoff, H.I. 1987), with permission of the Ansoff Family Trust; Figure 2.1 after *The 8 Steps to Strategic Success: Unleashing the Power of Engagement* (Van den Berg, G. and Pietersma, P. 2014), permission conveyed through Copyright Clearance Center, Inc. Republished with permission of Kogan Page; Figures 3.1 and 3.2 after The Business Model Canvas, **www.businessmodelgeneration.com**; Figures 4.1 and 4.2 after 'The TOWS matrix – A tool for situational analysis', *Long Range Planning* 15(2), pp. 54–66 (Weihrich, H. 1982), with permission from Elsevier; Figure 5.1 after 'The Balanced Scorecard: Measures that drive performance', *Harvard Business Review* 70(1), pp. 71–80 (Kaplan, R.S. and Norton, D.P. 1992), Copyright © 1992 by the Harvard Business School Publishing Corporation, all rights reserved. Reprinted by permission of Harvard Business Review; Figure 7.1 after *Competitive Advantage: Creating and Sustaining Superior Performance*, Free Press (Porter, M.E. 1985), Copyright © 1985, 1998 by Michael E. Porter, all rights reserved. Reproduced with the permission of Simon & Schuster Publishing Group, a Division of Simon and Schuster, Inc.; Figure 8.1 adapted from *Cost and Effect: Using Integrated Cost Systems to Drive Profitability and Performance*, Harvard Business School Press (Kaplan, R.S. and Cooper, R. 1998), Copyright © 1998 by the Harvard Business School Publishing Corporation, all rights reserved. Reproduced by permission of Harvard Business School Press; Figure 10.1 from *Marketing Management: Analysis, Planning, Implementation and Control*, 12th edn., Pearson Education (Kotler, P. and Keller, K.L. 2006), p. 27. Reprinted and electronically reproduced by permission of Pearson Education, Inc., Upper Saddle River, New Jersey; Figure 12.1 after 'Toward a theory of stakeholder identification and salience: Defining the principle of who and what really counts', *Academy of Management Review* 22(4), pp. 853–886 (Mitchell, R.K., Agle, B.R. and Wood, D.J. 1997). Republished with permission of the Academy of Management, permission conveyed through Copyright Clearance Center, Inc; Figure 18.1 after *Portfolio Management for New Products*, Perseus Books (Cooper, R.G., Edgett, S.J. and Kleinschmidt, E.J. 2002), p. 272, Exhibit 10.2, Copyright © Jan 4, 2002 Scott J. Edgett. Reprinted by permission of Basic Books, a member of the Perseus Books Group; Figure 19.1 after *A Force for Change: How Leadership Differs from Management*, Free Press (Kotter, J.P. 1990), Copyright © 1990 by John P. Kotter, Inc., all rights reserved. Reproduced with the permission of Simon & Schuster Publishing Group, a Division of Simon and Schuster, Inc., and the author; Figure 24.1 after *Cultures and Organizations: Software of the Mind*, 3rd revised edn., McGraw-Hill (Hofstede, G., Hofstede, G.J. and Minkov, M. 2010), © Geert Hofstede B.V., quoted with permission; Figure 25.1 after *The Seven Habits of Highly Effective People*, Simon & Schuster (Covey, S.R. 1989). Reprinted with permission of Franklin Covey Co.

In some instances we have been unable to trace the owners of copyright material, and we would appreciate any information that would enable us to do so.

Introduction

We are currently in the midst of a dynamic, disruptive period. Virtualisation and digitalisation are on the rise and business models based on physical bricks are under siege. Unfortunately, no management model, or group of models, can guarantee a manager or consultant the perfect solution to an organisational problem. At best they will provide a new way of seeing a situation that will enable positive change to take place as a result.

Although this book is about management models, in our consulting practice we often hear phrases like, 'We were well prepared to face this competitor, as our analysis with the Porter model has shown us that ...', or, 'We have been very busy lowering our prices to keep up in this climate of stiff price competition, but according to the BCG analysis, we ...', or even, 'The strategic dialogue model helped us to get strong support for this decision'. When events put the survival of the organisation at risk, and management is stuck running the day-to-day operational business, many people turn to management models for some common sense and information on why things turned out they way they have – as if management models provide the sole truth and the ultimate solution. To us, management models are nothing more and nothing less than useful tools – useful for problem solving, for analysis, for supporting and facilitating decision making and/ or for improving efficiency and the effectiveness of organisations and teams. In short, management models are, in our opinion, tools for resolving common problems and challenges in business.

Models can provide valuable insights and a sound framework for making appropriate business choices. Management models and theories can help managers and consultants to gain clarity in business by reducing the complexities and uncertainties involved – nothing more, but definitely nothing less.

The 2007–2014 crisis has made that very clear. Everybody knew that the crash in the financial system, the worldwide economic crisis, ongoing globalisation and the fact that the internet was here to stay, would mean huge challenges: different businesses, different business models and different demands on authenticity (practise what you preach), transparency (proof that you practise what you preach) and flexibility (be able to change your practice quickly). With the right type of management models, these events and their impact might have been seen upfront, and analysis and assessment of the underlying threats and possibilities of these events might help to identify what options and solutions are available to your organisation to deal with them.

However, the vast array of management models on offer can be bewildering, for managers and consultants alike. Being so commonly available, management models are used frequently. But all too often only a handful of worldwide well-known models are used – for instance, models from famous authors like Michael Porter or from large firms like McKinsey & Co or Boston Consulting Group. What about all those other models. Are they unknown? Probably not, but perhaps their application is unknown. Or it might not be clear what their purpose is or in which context they can best (or cannot) be used?

Based on our book *Key Management Models* (Pearson, 2014), we have selected 25 need-to-know management models for you. Each model is introduced with a description, followed by an explanation of why and when to use it, what the model does and what question(s) it helps you answer.

To put it clearly: this book is intended as a 'top 25' of popular management models, not as a prescription for 'good' management and organisation. It is intended as a selected anthology showing useful management models that have proven their value in practice to cope with the described challenges of our times.

It is again with both pleasure and pride that we present this compilation. We are confident that the managers and consultants who use it will possess the necessary maturity, intelligence and discernment to place the models we have included into perspective, and will use them to act on sound, creative, consistent management and advice.

We view this book as a means of giving expression to complexity, but also of making it more manageable, by providing 25 need-to-know models to simplify and visualise reality, so that management issues can be discussed based on a 'common language' and dealt with properly and swiftly. Use the models wisely in your own specific context: structuring reality is completely different from managing reality.

To all who read this book, we wish you lots of wisdom and pleasure. Above all, we hope you achieve many constructive results from applying the models to your own organisation.

How to use this book

For ease of use, each management model is described as follows:

- **The big picture** – the essence and purpose of the management model.
- **When to use it** – the usefulness and applicability of the management model.
- **How to use it** – a description of how to apply the management model using a step-by-step approach.
- **The final analysis** – the limitations of the management model and the potential pitfalls with regard to its use.
- **References** – an overview of literature sources on the origination of the management model with more information on (the use of) the management model.

Each entry includes one or more examples of how to apply the model and, where useful, includes an illustrative example which describes how the models can be used in a specific situation. Where relevant we also refer to alternative, but equally applicable, models that are included in this book, but it is certainly not our claim to be exhaustive or exclusive.

There are many more models and methods available than those described in this book – you can find them on numerous websites or in other books on business management (including FT Publishing's *Key Management Models* (3rd edition), *Key Management Ratios* and *Key Strategy Tools*, and books by Berenschot consultants).

In the end it should be you who picks the management models that are most appropriate to your situation, as each model should help you to organise and interpret the information you regard as relevant and help you to understand what choices you have to make based on that information.

Top 10 do's and don'ts of using management models

Top 5 do's

1. Do connect your mind, heart and gut feeling

Useful insights gained from business analytics and data crunching may help you to understand the context and content of your business (mind), but without passion (heart), the motivation to pursue the strategic goals of your organisation will be missing. Moreover, if the direction, decision or course of action doesn't feel good (gut feeling), your leadership will lack conviction and the organisation will fail to follow. So, decisions must be made based on a solid connection between mind, heart and gut feeling. The rich variety of management models available, ranging from engineering approaches to social sciences and psychology, can help you in this.

2. Do take time to discuss outcomes

Management models are designed to resolve common problems and challenges in business. Unfortunately, no management model, or group of models, can deal with an organisational problem in itself. Management models can help by providing a structured and logical view on the situation or even a new way of seeing it. It is then the interpretation and shared understanding of this view that provides the valuable insights and the sound basis for making appropriate business choices.

3. Do use management models as a means, not as an end

Management models and theories can help managers and consultants to gain clarity in business by reducing complexity and uncertainty. They can overcome differences in perception and abstraction and provide comprehensiveness. To make optimal use of management models, make sure you know what you want to achieve and use the management model for this. Define the questions you want to answer. Then pick the (most) appropriate model and use the outcomes as input, but not the only input, for your decision making.

4. Do use models accurately

Many management models are founded in academic research. They have been 'proven' using statistical analysis and/or quantitative research. Some models have a mathematical basis, even if this is not obvious at first. As most models are introduced with very extensive elaboration on their origin and on their intended use (by its inventor or proprietary owner), be well advised to use the management model as it is intended. This will maximise the validity of the outcomes of the management model and thus will maximise the usefulness of the management model (and its outcomes) in your own business situation.

5. Do use models freely

Many models have been 'invented' in specific situations and are then presented as widely applicable to many situations. Many other management models have been introduced as generic models that can be applied to any situation. This makes it clear that to effectively make use of management models you should know which model is appropriate in which situation. On the other hand, to make the best use of a management model it might be necessary to customise the use of the model, or even the management model itself, to your needs and your situation. Please feel free when needed and come up with your own model! It might even be suited to apply generically and become the next key management model.

Top 5 don'ts

1. Don't assume the outcomes are obvious to everybody

Some management models may be familiar to some colleagues, but probably not all. This is not surprising – there are so many management models in many fields of expertise. You would not expect a psychologist, who has never worked in R&D or an (industrial) operations department, to know about stage-gating. Nor would you expect an engineer to know about competing values. When introducing and using management models make sure you explain the model clearly and thoroughly to all involved. Pay particular attention to how the model works. Don't hide any shortcomings of the model from your colleagues – always let them know what areas it can be helpful in and where it is of no use at all.

2. Don't make outcomes absolute

Some management models are strongly data driven – for instance models in finance or in operations often have a quantitative character. However, the management models function according to the adage: garbage in, garbage out. That means that a management model cannot compensate for or correct any incorrect data that is analysed with the model. When using models with a strong quantitative aspect, be thorough and precise about the data that you select for analysis.

3. Don't get into paralysis by analysis

Most management models can help you to find opportunities for your organisation or situation. Management and directors often have a 'risk-oriented mindset'. Don't be tempted to pursue the last digits after the comma and keep on analysing. If you keep on analysing you might drown in information, and fail to gain the critical insight you need in order to take a decision which will make you keeping on analysing, etc. Make sure you define how you intend to use the management model in terms of quality, completeness and depth.

4. Don't overestimate model logic

Some management models can provide very clear and pointed outcomes. However, these outcomes should only provide you with a single input into your decision making. They are not the absolute truth but only semi- or quasi-mathematical answers. A management model can only lead to systemic logical outcomes or straightforward suggestions to an approach, but it takes a human decision maker to come up with acceptable exceptions.

5. Don't underestimate the power of visualisation

One of the benefits of using proven management models is that they are universally accepted and recognised. Management models, both those that provide suggestions for an approach and those that help with (quantitative) analysis, can help you present your findings, decisions or suggested approach in a structured and logical manner. This often is very helpful in decision making. Especially as many management models also have visually attractive representations. These are themselves very helpful in decision making, as everybody gets the same information in the same structured way from the visualisation, and is thus forced to the same interpretation in the same language. So don't underestimate the power of using a management model to get a positive outcome.

part
one

Strategy

Ansoff's matrix and product market grid

- **Why use it?** Ansoff's matrix and product market grid provides a structured way to determine the scope and direction of a firm's strategic development.

- **What does it do?** These models help to analyse and plan a company's strategy for future growth.

- **When to use it?** The Ansoff product/market grid and the Ansoff cube can be used as a framework to identify direction and opportunities for corporate growth.

- **What question will it help you answer?** What are our strategic opportunities for future growth?

The big picture

The Ansoff product/market grid offers a logical way of determining the scope and direction of a firm's strategic development in the marketplace. The firm's strategic development consists of two related types of strategy: portfolio strategy and competitive strategy.

The portfolio strategy specifies the objectives for each of the firm's product/market combinations. It points to the dots on the horizon. The competitive strategy specifies the route to take to reach those objectives.

In the Ansoff product/market grid setting, the objectives (portfolio strategy) were introduced as choosing a growth vector, specifying the ultimate future scope of business. The growth vector is expressed in two dimensions: products and markets (Figure 1.1).

Later, Ansoff introduced the geographical growth vector, replacing the growth vector from his product/market grid (Figure 1.2). The geographical growth vector has three dimensions, which the firm can use to define its desired future business scope:

- **the market need** (e.g. need for personal transportation or need for amplification of electric signals);
- **the product/service technology** (e.g. integrated circuit technology);
- **the market geography** (e.g. regions or nation states).

These three dimensions together form a cube. They offer a variety of combinations and strategic directions for a firm. Extreme choices are on the one hand to continue serving current regions with existing technologies to fulfil traditional needs or on the other hand to enter new regions with new technologies to fulfil new needs.

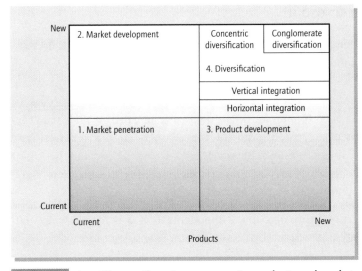

Figure 1.1 Ansoff's growth vector components: products and markets

Source: after Ansoff (1987)

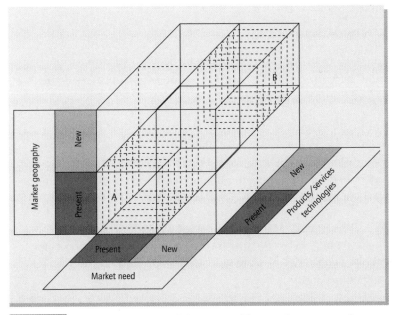

Figure 1.2 Ansoff's dimensions of the geographic growth vector: market need; products/services and technologies; and market geography

Source: after Ansoff (1987)

When to use it

Deciding a direction and a strategy for corporate growth depends upon a number of factors, including: the level of risk involved; the current set of products and markets; and whether the organisation wants to develop new or existing products or markets. In order to plan for the future in a systematic way, it is vital that managers understand the gap between the firm's current and desired positions. The Ansoff product/market grid and the Ansoff cube can be used as a framework to identify the direction of and opportunities for corporate growth.

Ansoff introduced four components that cover the portfolio strategy and help specify the desired future business scope:

1 Geographical growth vector
2 Competitive advantage
3 Synergies
4 Strategic flexibility.

The geographical growth vector can be determined with Ansoff's cube, by connecting the current scope of business with the desired future business scope.

A competitive advantage is needed both to enable the chosen scope and to be able to sustain a route towards it. The competitive advantage can be anything from a core competence or a patented technology to offering better after-sales service to clients than your competitors.

As a third strategy component, Ansoff suggests taking account of the synergy between the firm's competencies. This not only enables economies of scale but can also strengthen the firm's competitive position.

The fourth, and final, strategic component is the strategic flexibility. It is aimed at minimising the impact of unforeseen events and seeks to discard all unnecessary 'ballast'.

The four components are interlinked. Optimising one of the components is likely to depress the firm's performance in the others. In particular, maximising synergies is very likely to reduce flexibility. The process of selecting and balancing the strategic objectives is a complex matter.

How to use it

To use the product/market grid in practice, an organisation must first assess its existing product–market combinations and corresponding levels of competitive advantage. Then, its desired future business scope must be chosen as the geographical growth vector within the Ansoff cube.

Next, the feasibility of the chosen scope and direction should be assessed, with an analysis of the combination of the intended direction and extent of corporate growth and the firm's distinctive competitive advantages (core competencies). Not only should there be the means that enable the chosen scope, those means should also provide the firm with a sustainable competitive advantage.

Then, synergies have to be found and/or created either by making use of an existing outstanding competence (aggressive synergy strategy) or by developing or acquiring the necessary competence (defensive synergy strategy).

Finally, strategic flexibility has to be attained. This can be done externally to the firm through diversification of the firm's geographic scope, needs served and technologies so that a surprising change in any one of the strategic business areas does not produce a seriously damaging impact on the firm's performance. Alternatively, it can be attained by basing the firm's activities on resources and capabilities that are easily transferable.

A shortcut in determining the strategic objectives is to derive them from the strategic requirements of three archetype firms:

- **An operating company** will focus on synergies and a relatively narrowly focused geographical growth vector. Its investments are often irreversible, have long lead times and will often be in research and development (R&D) or physical assets. It must be able to anticipate change and minimise the changes of making bad decisions. Synergies will often be created around core competencies.

- **A conglomerate firm** will focus on flexibility. Its strategy would have no synergy or geographical growth vector. Instead it would include enough flexibility to be protected from strategic surprises or discontinuities in the environment of one or more of its subsidiaries.

- **An investment fund** can only focus on flexibility. It will have widely diversified holdings. Such firms seldom have the depth of knowledge of individual industries to enable them to seek a specific competitive advantage.

In fact, these 'pure form' firms do not exist. There are no stereo-types, as there are numerous shadings of characteristics. There are different degrees of integration in synergistic companies: some companies act as conglomerates in some parts and are synergistic in others, and some investment firms do have specialised knowl-edge of certain industries. Each firm will have to determine its own strategic objectives (portfolio strategy).

Next, a competitive strategy is adopted to determine the distinc-tive approach to succeed in reaching the chosen objectives in the strategic portfolio strategy (the path forward). Based on the origi-nal product/market grid, four generic competitive strategies were identified:

- **Market penetration** (current product/current market) – sell more of the same products and services in existing markets. This growth vector indicates growth through increase in market share for the present product/markets.

▓ **Market development** (current product/new market) – sell more of the same products and services in new markets.

▓ **Product development** (new product/current market) – sell new products and services into existing markets. This growth vector means growth by developing new products to replace or complement existing products.

▓ **Diversification** (new product/new market) – sell new products and services into new markets.

Also, depending on how 'different' the new product and the new market are, a variety of more specific growth vectors were identified within the diversification quadrant:

▓ **Vertical integration** – an organisation acquires or moves into suppliers' or customers' areas of expertise to ensure the supply or use of its own products and services.

▓ **Horizontal diversification** – new (technologically unrelated) products are introduced to current markets.

▓ **Concentric diversification** – new products, closely related to current products, are introduced into current and/or new markets.

▓ **Conglomerate diversification** – completely new, technologically unrelated products are introduced into new markets.

There are, of course, different roads that lead to Rome. The generic competitive strategies can only do little to answer the question of which competitive strategy would be the most beneficial. Each firm will have to determine its own strategic objectives (portfolio strategy) and its own strategic direction (competitive strategy).

The final analysis

Despite its age, Ansoff's work remains valid and is used a great deal in practice. Although the product/market grid is primarily used in its original form, it still offers a good framework for describing product/market opportunities and strategic options. It forms a good basis for further exploration and strategic dialogue.

What is groundbreaking, however, are the amendments Ansoff himself made to his own work. With the perspective of more than 20 years' experience, he concluded that his own, very well known product/market grid did not reflect reality enough and he introduced a different approach to corporate strategy. Revisiting all of Ansoff's work makes it clear that some of today's favourite management tools originate from his models.

References

Ansoff, H.I. (1984) *Implanting Strategic Management*. Englewood Cliffs: Prentice Hall.

Ansoff, H. I. (1987) *Corporate Strategy* (revised edition). London: Penguin Books.

Ansoff, H.I. (1988) *New Corporate Strategy*. New York: John Wiley and Sons.

2

Strategic dialogue

■ **Why use it?** The strategic dialogue is a generic eight-step model for formulating and implementing strategy that is based on engagement with key stakeholders: what the organisation can and will do is not invented in an ivory tower, but is developed and implemented in dialogue with key external and internal partners and stakeholders.

■ **What does it do?** The model treats strategy as an integral process of formulation and implementation. It focuses on content and process: doing the right things and doing things right. It is an iterative process with an approach that leads to making clear strategic choices with the support of key stakeholders.

■ **When to use it?** The strategic dialogue can be used as a systematic approach to strategy in situations where both the formulation and implementation of a realistic and supported strategic plan is needed.

■ **What question will it help you answer?** How should I organise my strategy process to maximise the chances for strategic success?

The big picture

The strategic dialogue is a generic eight-step model for formulating and implementing strategy (Figure 2.1). It focuses on content and process: doing the right things and doing things right. It is an iterative process with an approach that leads to choices while leaving room to keep options open. And it is an approach – the name 'strategic dialogue' says it all – that is based on engagement with key stakeholders: what the organisation can and will do are not formulated in an ivory tower, but rather in dialogue with key external partners and stakeholders, and these are explored and discussed with internal stakeholders. However, a dialogue doesn't imply a democracy: those responsible will still have the final say and have to make the strategic choices.

In a strategy process, there are three critical success factors:

- A good understanding of the **context** of the strategy definition: without shared understanding of cause, necessity and ambition, a company trying to formulate its strategy is drifting. And without knowing where you stand, there is no way to set a course.

- An adequate use of **content** in terms of quality, completeness and depth – a thorough analysis with appropriate models and instruments to obtain a complete understanding of the possibilities and impossibilities of the organisation and of the environment in which it is active. A thorough analysis is the basis for finding the right strategic options.

- An effective and inspiring **process** based on engagement: who are involved at what moment in time, what are the roles, and how is participation organised? In other words: applying the correct methods of engagement. These help to increase the intrinsic level of understanding, stimulate creativity and develop ideas.

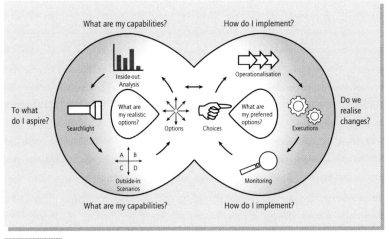

Figure 2.1 Strategic dialogue   Source: after Van den Berg and Pietersma (2014)

For strategic success, organisations will have to understand the essence of context, the essence of content and the essence of the process. Organising both strategy formulation and strategy implementation processes as a dialogue will lead to strategic success. The strategic dialogue presumes that strategic success is the result of the formula:

Formulation × Mobilisation × Realisation

That is to say, strategic success comes from successful strategy formulation multiplied by mobilisation of the right people times successful strategy realisation (or implementation).

Formulation

Many companies devote most of their attention to the F of formulation. They formulate a strategy that, if correct, shows them the way amid the uncertainties of current and future markets. It could lead to the perfect plan. And then it is 'only' a matter of perfect execution. All too often, however, strategic plans are not flawless. It is difficult to make the right choices up front for unforeseen future developments. Often choices made – if they really are made in the first place – do not always reflect a combination of thorough analysis and sound entrepreneurship. And often the strategy states what the company will do, but not what the company will stop doing (which is often inherent in making choices). Emphasis on formulation is no guarantee for a consistent execution of strategy, nor for a consistent interpretation by all involved.

Realisation

Next to formulation, it is the R of realisation that typically receives the most attention in strategy processes. Sometimes there are elaborate and detailed implementation plans, which are as comprehensive as an encyclopaedia, and sometimes these are only fragmentary. Most of the time there is some kind of implementation plan, and attention will be given to communication and progress. Milestones and required breakthroughs in the implementation plan are monitored and periodically scheduled on the management agenda (however, they are often not properly addressed, as operational fires must be extinguished first). But even if there is a brilliant strategy with elaborate implementation plans and well-managed change projects, all too often everyone is still surprised that the strategy is not working and does not deliver what they had expected.

Mobilisation

The demands faced by companies in the twenty-first century are structurally different from before and this will be (or should be) reflected in the strategy process. Strategy processes have (or have to) become more agile and decisive. Strategy inherently is about the long term, but nowadays the pressure from banks and shareholders to achieve results in the short term is great. The tolerance for mistakes and risks remains low. Adjustments must be made instantly. You must therefore focus more than ever on the third variable: the M of mobilisation. This is about organising involvement and engagement in the process of both strategy formulation and strategy implementation. In short, it is about engaging key business partners and both external and internal stakeholders to get their understanding of and support for (or even buy-in on) your strategy.

When to use it

The strategic dialogue is a systematic approach to strategy formulation to be used in situations where both the formulation and implementation of a realistic and supported strategic plan are needed. It was originally developed as a methodology to overcome generic pitfalls that were frequently found during strategy formulation. These pitfalls are to be avoided in any strategy process and involve three aspects of the strategy formulation process: the scope of the process; the execution of the process; and the decision-making in the process. These aspects, and a description of some of the pitfalls, are shown in the following table.

Aspect	Pitfall	Description
Scope	'Me too'	Blindly following the most important (or annoying) competitor.
	'The grass is always greener'	Getting carried away with seemingly attractive new initiatives or possibilities and forgetting to make rational considerations.
	'Collective truth'	Too much reasoning from a collective vision, being too caught up with the organisation's own dynamics, and too little analysis.
	'We've always done it this way'	Holding on too rigidly on to past experiences.
	'We know what they want'	Making assumptions on markets and customers instead of doing a thorough analysis.

▶

Aspect	Pitfall	Description
Execution	'An elite activity'	Involving top management only and not the rest of the organisation.
	'No time to discuss'	Taking too little time for the process.
	'The controller as strategist'	Presenting budget adjustments ('last year's plan +5%') as strategy.
	'Paralysis by analysis'	Getting stuck in continuous analysis into the last digits behind the comma, often driven by a 'risk-averse mindset'.
	'Talk about them, not with them'	Engaging key external and internal stakeholders is experienced as difficult, inappropriate and/or inconvenient.
Choices	'It's all about the money'	Dominance of financial considerations (bottom line), making strategy more like an investment prospectus.
	'The hockey stick effect'	Placing ambitions over analysis, leading to overly optimistic long-term prognosis.
	'Let's make a compromise'	Trying to keep everybody happy and avoiding to make real choices
	'There is only one boss...'	Top management makes every decision (and wonders why nobody gets it or follows through on it).
	'Another good plan (for the file)'	Not putting the strategy into action.

We emphasise that the context or situation in which a new strategy is to be formulated affects both the content of the strategy and the process of formulating the strategy. This, of course, also holds for a strategy process with the strategic dialogue model. The scope and depth of the strategy process with the strategic dialogue model are also highly dependent on the specific contexts. This includes such contexts as restructuring, mergers or acquisitions and external disruptions (new technologies etc.). In each of these situations, compromises must be made between different aspects in the strategy process, as circumstances require specific demands. It may be that there is only a little time available, and the lead time will therefore be limited. It can also prevent the requirements of confidentiality limiting the group of people involved in expressing themselves. The nature of a specific situation determines the strategy process, sometimes creating more constraints than for a 'regular' strategy process.

How to use it

The strategic dialogue model is an integrated methodology of strategy formulation and implementation which has been developed on the basis of practical experience. It is not a one-size-fits-all standard prescription on how to do strategy, but it's a generic approach that you can customise to your organisation and circumstances. Every company and every environment are different and require a customised approach. The strategic dialogue model offers an iterative process which is applicable to a multitude of situations and strategic issues. In the strategic dialogue model, we identified eight distinct steps, each with distinctive purposes, scope and activities:

- **Searchlight.** The setting of the process of strategy formulation and implementation and finding a shared ambition and business scope.

- **Outside-in: Scenarios.** The mapping of potential strategic positions from plausible future business environments.

- **Inside-out: Analysis.** The exploration of strategic options based on the abilities and limitations in the company.

- **Options.** The translation of analytical information to insights and, from there, to generating strategic options.

- **Choice.** The estimation of the risks and feasibility of the various options, leading to the choice of strategy.

- **Operationalisation.** Making an implementation plan, setting the implementation process in detail and cashing in on 'quick wins'.

- **Execution.** The actual implementation of plans, policies and actions for change.

- **Monitoring.** The assessment of ongoing developments in the environment and organisational performance in relation to the strategy and strategic goals.

In each of the eight steps, other management models can be used for analysis, design or interaction. These are not equally important in every situation, nor is there a prescribed list of models to use in one or more of the steps. To get a clearer view of which ones to use, and when, see the references at the end of this chapter.

The schematic of the strategic dialogue model has the shape of two circles linked together: the process of formulation and of implementation (see Figure 2.1). These two circles together also form a lemniscate – the symbol for infinity – representing the integrated and iterative character of our approach to strategy. It depicts how everything is connected to everything else through logical links. Ideally, the strategy process will go through all eight steps of the model (an entire cycle) from left to right in the figure. The process of developing a mission statement, vision and strategy is described in the left-hand cycle. This process is fluid, interactive and creative. In the middle, the actual process of selection of strategic options takes place. This is where different options are weighed and choices are made. In the right-hand cycle, the emphasis is on the realisation and implementation of the choices made. This process is more rigid and action-oriented.

The final analysis

Formulating a successful strategy depends upon the quality of content and the method of implementation. However, of equal importance is the way in which the process is organised and the way the results are communicated to all parties. Efficient organisation and effective dialogue will greatly increase the success of the implementation phase. A number of factors are critical to get right when first setting up the process, in order to optimise the chances of delivering successful results:

- Determine who is to be involved, and which roles they are to assume during the strategy formulation process.
- Decide how to organise enthusiasm and buy-in for the strategy with the rest of the organisation – a plan without any commitment from those supposed to execute it is unlikely to succeed.
- Assess the quality of the team members' input with regard to both the analyses and the vision. Consider their willingness to think about the future in a systematic and fundamental way.
- Decide which other models and instruments would be of value as part of the process.
- Decide how to communicate with non-participants about and during the process. This becomes increasingly important once the results become visible.
- Include processes to ensure that agreed procedures are adhered to, by all those involved, especially during the implementation phase.

References

Van den Berg, G. and Pietersma, P. (2012) *The Grand Book on Strategy*. Den Haag: SDU [in Dutch: *Het Groot Strategieboek*].

Van den Berg, G. and Pietersma, P. (2014) *The 8 Steps to Strategic Success: Unleashing the Power of Engagement*. London: Kogan Page.

3

Business model canvas

- **Why use it?** The business model canvas is particularly suitable to develop new and/or alternative business models. It is a hands-on tool that fosters understanding and creativity.

- **What does it do?** The model provides a canvas to describe, visualise, develop and explore business models. The template is based on nine basic building blocks, which can show at a glance how a company does its business and earns money.

- **When to use it?** The model can be used to generate new business models and to foster ideas for and new ways of doing business. It is also a perfect tool to analyse the existing business model of your organisation and find areas for improvement.

- **What question will it help you answer?** What is the best business model for my organisation: how can my organisation create and deliver value?

The big picture

The business model canvas as introduced by Alex Osterwalder (2010) describes the possible rationale of how an organisation creates, delivers and preserves value. It provides a canvas to describe, visualise, develop and explore business models. On the basis of nine basic building blocks, one can see at a glance how a company does its business and earns money (see Figure 3.1). The model is highly visual and shows how the building blocks interlock. It provides a common language to discuss current and (potential) future business models.

When to use it

The business model canvas has become popular thanks to its highly visual, integrated view, showing how a business actually functions. It is a perfect tool – as it was originally intended – for generating new business models and ideas for and new ways of doing business. But it is also a perfect tool to analyse the existing business of your organisation and find areas for improvement.

Figure 3.1 Business model canvas   Source: www.businessmodelgeneration.com

The model can also be used in strategic decision-making for your own organisation. It can provide inspiration and/or strategic insights by analysing your competitors' businesses. It can also be very helpful in making strategic options to choose from more tangible. With the business model canvas, alternative business models can be developed or completely new business models conceived that had previously not been considered.

How to use it

The business model canvas consists of nine generic building blocks:

1 **Customer segments.** For whom do we create value? Who are our most important customers? What characterises our clients? How can we segment our markets?

2 **Value proposition.** What value do we provide our customers? What customer problems do we solve? How does that vary between customer segments?

3 **Servicing model or channels.** How do we (want to) reach our customers? What are customer demands on delivery and service? What works best, what is cost-effective? How does my supply chain look?

4 **Customer relationships.** What relationship do customers in each segment expect? Which service level is required for which type of customer? Does the customer have a relationship with us too or are they just transaction-oriented?

5 **Revenues.** How do we earn from our customers? What do they pay for? How much do customers pay now or how much are they willing to pay? How do we generate income with each transaction?

6 **Key resources.** Which resources are necessary to create and deliver for the value proposition, the channels and the

customer relationship? Do we have unique resources and/or exclusive access to resources?

7 **Key activities.** Which activities are needed to create and deliver for the value proposition, to use the channels, to foster relationships and to reach the customers? Do we have unique activities? What do we do that is different from our competitors?

8 **Key partners.** Who are our main partners? What resources do they have and what activities do our partners do (better than us) that enable us to deliver value to our customers?

9 **Cost structure.** What are the costs of creating and delivering our added value to our customers? Which of our (or our partner's) important resources are the most expensive? Which main activities cost the most? How do we incur costs with each transaction?

When using the business model canvas, the first step is to print out an enlarged blank canvas (see Figure 3.2). This can then be used as a drawing board on which groups of people can together start sketching and writing, or sticking on Post-it notes. Each of the nine building blocks are to be considered and discussed. There are also many digital tools available for the business model canvas (an app for tablet computers, an online toolbox and a serious game).

The final analysis

A pitfall of the business model canvas is that the analysis of its nine building blocks is often based on assumptions rather than facts. Particularly poor knowledge about existing customers but also about new segments often leads to unsubstantiated assumptions. A second pitfall is that a substantiation of a strategic option is prematurely regarded as the best or only business model for that strategic option (too much concrete, insufficient exploration). The business model canvas is particularly suitable for creating multiple, alternative models. It is a hands-on tool that fosters understanding and creativity.

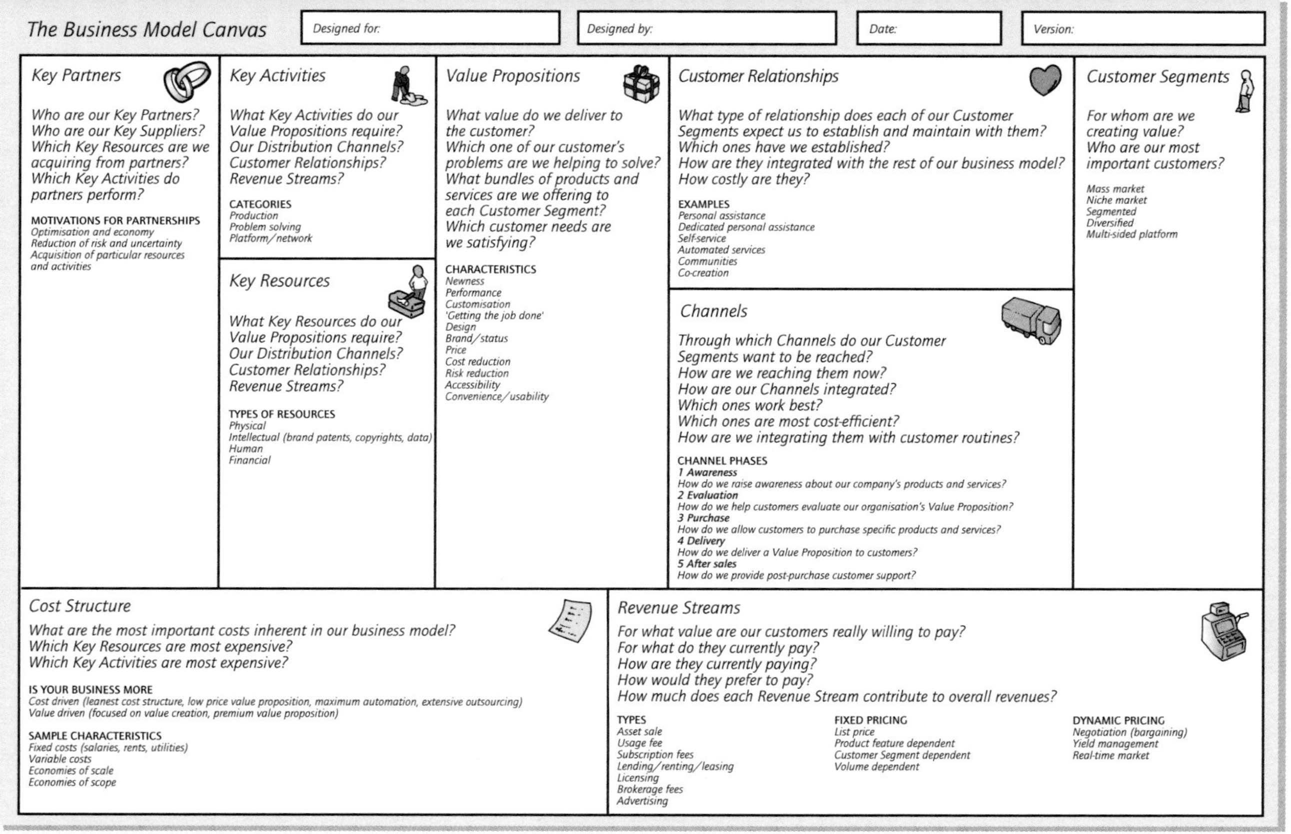

The Business Model Canvas

Designed for: Designed by: Date: Version:

Key Partners

Who are our Key Partners?
Who are our Key Suppliers?
Which Key Resources are we
acquiring from partners?
Which Key Activities do
partners perform?

MOTIVATIONS FOR PARTNERSHIPS
Optimisation and economy
Reduction of risk and uncertainty
Acquisition of particular resources
and activities

Key Activities

What Key Activities do our
Value Propositions require?
Our Distribution Channels?
Customer Relationships?
Revenue Streams?

CATEGORIES
Production
Problem solving
Platform/network

Key Resources

What Key Resources do our
Value Propositions require?
Our Distribution Channels?
Customer Relationships?
Revenue Streams?

TYPES OF RESOURCES
Physical
Intellectual (brand patents, copyrights, data)
Human
Financial

Value Propositions

What value do we deliver to
the customer?
Which one of our customer's
problems are we helping to solve?
What bundles of products and
services are we offering to
each Customer Segment?
Which customer needs are
we satisfying?

CHARACTERISTICS
Newness
Performance
Customisation
'Getting the job done'
Design
Brand/status
Price
Cost reduction
Risk reduction
Accessibility
Convenience/usability

Customer Relationships

What type of relationship does each of our Customer
Segments expect us to establish and maintain with them?
Which ones have we established?
How are they integrated with the rest of our business model?
How costly are they?

EXAMPLES
Personal assistance
Dedicated personal assistance
Self-service
Automated services
Communities
Co-creation

Channels

Through which Channels do our Customer
Segments want to be reached?
How are we reaching them now?
How are our Channels integrated?
Which ones work best?
Which ones are most cost-efficient?
How are we integrating them with customer routines?

CHANNEL PHASES
1 Awareness
How do we raise awareness about our company's products and services?
2 Evaluation
How do we help customers evaluate our organisation's Value Proposition?
3 Purchase
How do we allow customers to purchase specific products and services?
4 Delivery
How do we deliver a Value Proposition to customers?
5 After sales
How do we provide post-purchase customer support?

Customer Segments

For whom are we
creating value?
Who are our most
important customers?

Mass market
Niche market
Segmented
Diversified
Multi-sided platform

Cost Structure

What are the most important costs inherent in our business model?
Which Key Resources are most expensive?
Which Key Activities are most expensive?

IS YOUR BUSINESS MORE
Cost driven (leanest cost structure, low price value proposition, maximum automation, extensive outsourcing)
Value driven (focused on value creation, premium value proposition)

SAMPLE CHARACTERISTICS
Fixed costs (salaries, rents, utilities)
Variable costs
Economies of scale
Economies of scope

Revenue Streams

For what value are our customers really willing to pay?
For what do they currently pay?
How are they currently paying?
How would they prefer to pay?
How much does each Revenue Stream contribute to overall revenues?

TYPES
Asset sale
Usage fee
Subscription fees
Lending/renting/leasing
Licensing
Brokerage fees
Advertising

FIXED PRICING
List price
Product feature dependent
Customer Segment dependent
Volume dependent

DYNAMIC PRICING
Negotiation (bargaining)
Yield management
Real-time market

Source: www.businessmodelgeneration.com

Figure 3.2 The business model canvas

References

Business Model Generation website:
http://www.businessmodelgeneration.com

Osterwalder, A. (2004) *The Business Model Ontology – A Proposition in a Design Science Approach.* University of Lausanne.

Osterwalder, A. and Pigneur, Y. (2010) *Business Model Generation: A Handbook for Visionaries, Game Changers and Challengers.* Hoboken, New Jersey: John Wiley & Sons.

4

SWOT analysis

- **Why use it?** SWOT analysis provides helpful information for matching resources and capabilities to the competitive environment in which the organisation operates.

- **What does it do?** A SWOT analysis is a valuable self-assessment tool for management. Comprising four elements – strengths, weaknesses, opportunities and threats – it may appear deceptively simple. In fact, deciding what the strengths and weaknesses of a company are, as well as assessing the likelihood and impact of the opportunities and threats in the external environment, is far more complex than it appears at first sight.

- **When to use it?** The model can be used as an instrument for devising and selecting strategy, and is applicable in any decision-making situation.

■ **What questions will it help you answer?** What are my organisation's primary, or urgent, strategic issues and what are the actions the organisation has to take? Should the company focus on using its strengths to capitalise on opportunities, or on acquiring strengths in order to capture opportunities? Moreover, should the company try actively to minimise weaknesses and avoid threats?

The big picture

Any company undertaking strategic planning must at some point assess its strengths and weaknesses. When combined with an inventory of opportunities and threats within or beyond the company's environment, the company is making a so-called SWOT analysis (or TOWS analysis), establishing its current position in the light of its strengths, weaknesses, opportunities and threats (Figure 4.1).

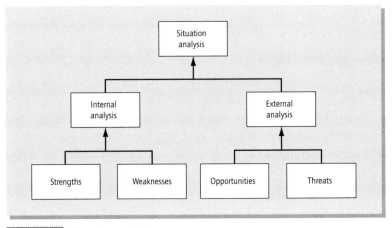

Figure 4.1 Situation analysis

Source: after Weihrich (1982)

When to use it

The SWOT analysis provides helpful information for matching resources and capabilities to the competitive environment in which the organisation operates. The model can be used as an instrument for devising and selecting strategy, and is equally applicable in any decision-making situation, provided the desired objective has been clearly defined.

How to use it

The first step in carrying out a SWOT analysis is to identify the company's strengths, weaknesses, opportunities and threats. A scan of the internal and external environments is therefore an important part of the process. Strengths and weaknesses are internal factors. They are the skills and assets (or lack of them) that are intrinsic to the company and which add to or detract from the value of the company, relative to competitive forces. Opportunities and threats, however, are external factors: they are not created by the company, but emerge due to the activity of competitors, and changes in the market dynamics.

- **Strengths.** What does the company do well? For example, does the company benefit from an experienced sales force or easy access to raw materials? Do people buy the company's products (partly) because of its brand(s) or reputation? Note: a growing market or new products are not classed as strengths – they are opportunities.

- **Weaknesses.** These are the things that a company lacks or does not do well. Although weaknesses are often seen as the logical 'inverse' of the company's threats, the company's lack of strength in a particular discipline or market is not necessarily a relative weakness, provided that (potential) competitors also lack this particular strength.

Strengths and weaknesses can be measured with the help of an internal or external audit, e.g. through benchmarking (see also Chapter 6). Opportunities and threats occur because of external macro-environmental forces such as demographic, economic, technological, political, legal, social and cultural dynamics, as well as external industry-specific environmental forces such as customers, competitors, distribution channels and suppliers.

- **Opportunities.** Could the company benefit from any technological developments or demographic changes taking place, or could the demand for its products or services increase as a result of successful partnerships? Could assets be used in other ways? For example, current products could be introduced to new markets, or R&D could be turned into cash by licensing concepts, technologies or selling patents. There are many perceived opportunities; whether they are real depends upon the extent and level of detail included in the market analysis.

■ **Threats.** One company's opportunity may well be another company's threat. Changes in regulations, substitute technologies and other forces in the competitive field may pose serious threats, resulting, for example, in lower sales, higher cost of operations, higher cost of capital, inability to break even, shrinking margins or profitability, and rates of return dropping significantly below market expectations.

After the internal and external analysis, the results can be placed in a so-called *confrontation matrix* (Figure 4.2). In this matrix, the strengths, weaknesses, opportunities and threats can be listed and

Company Date:	O1	O2	O3	O4	O5	T1	T2	T3	T4	T5	TOTAL
TOTAL											100
S1											
S2											
S3											
S4											
S5											
W1											
W2											
W3											
W4											
W5											

Figure 4.2 **The confrontation matrix**   Source: adapted from Weihrich (1982)

combined. Then points can be given to each of the combinations: the more important they are, the more points are awarded. This confrontation leads to an identification of the organisation's primary, and often urgent, strategic issues.

The next step is to evaluate the actions the company has to take based on its SWOT analysis. Should the company focus on using its strengths to capitalise on opportunities, or acquire strengths in order to capture opportunities? Moreover, should the company try actively to minimise weaknesses and avoid threats? (See Figure 4.3.)

	Strengths (S)	Weaknesses (W)
Opportunities (O)	SO strategies *Use strengths to take advantage of opportunities*	WO strategies *Take advantage of opportunities by overcoming weaknesses or making them relevant*
Threats (T)	ST strategies *Use strengths to avoid threats*	WT strategies *Minimise weaknesses and avoid threats*

Figure 4.3 SWOT analysis

'SO' and 'WT' strategies are straightforward. A company should do what it is good at when the opportunity arises, and avoid businesses for which it does not have the competencies. Less obvious and much more risky are 'WO' strategies. When a company decides to take on an opportunity despite not having the required strengths, it must:

- develop the required strengths;
- buy or borrow the required strengths; or
- outmanoeuvre the competition.

In essence, companies that use 'ST' strategies will 'buy or bust' their way out of trouble. This happens when big players fend off smaller ones by means of expensive price wars, insurmountable marketing budgets or multiple channel promotions. Some companies use scenario planning to try to anticipate and thus be prepared for this type of future threat.

The steps in the commonly used three-phase SWOT analysis process are:

Phase 1: Detect strategic issues

1 Identify external issues relevant to the firm's strategic position in the industry and the general environment at large, with the understanding that opportunities and threats are factors that management cannot influence directly.

2 Identify internal issues relevant to the firm's strategic position.

3 Analyse and rank the external issues according to probability and impact.

4 List the key strategic issues and factors inside or outside the organisation that significantly affect the long-term competitive position in the SWOT matrix.

Phase 2: Determine the strategy

5 Identify the firm's strategic fit, given its internal capabilities and external environment.

6 Formulate alternative strategies to address key issues.

7 Place the alternative strategies in one of the four quadrants in the SWOT matrix:

(i) SO - internal strengths combined with external opportunities is the ideal mix, but requires an understanding of how the internal strengths can support weaknesses in other areas;

(ii) WO - internal weaknesses combined with opportunities must be judged on investment effectiveness to determine whether the gain is worth the effort of buying or developing the internal capability;

(iii) ST – internal strengths combined with external threats requires knowing the merit of adapting the organisation in order to change the threat into an opportunity;

(iv) WT – internal weaknesses combined with threats creates a worst-case scenario. Radical changes such as divestment are required.

8 Develop additional strategies for any remaining 'blind spots' in the SWOT matrix.

9 Select an appropriate strategy.

Phase 3: Implement and monitor strategy

10 Develop an action plan to implement the SWOT strategy.

11 Assign responsibilities and budgets.

12 Monitor progress.

13 Start the review process from the beginning.

The final analysis

A SWOT analysis is a valuable self-assessment tool for management. The elements – strengths, weaknesses, opportunities and threats – appear deceptively simple, but, in fact, deciding what the strengths and weaknesses of a company are, as well as assessing the impact and probability of the opportunities and threats in the external environment, is far more complex than it looks at first sight. Furthermore, beyond classification of the SWOT elements, the model offers no assistance with the tricky task of translating the findings into strategic alternatives. The inherent risk of making incorrect assumptions when assessing the SWOT elements often causes management to dither when it comes to choosing between various strategic alternatives, frequently resulting in unnecessary and/or undesirable delays.

References

Abell, D.F. and Hammond, J.S. (1979) *Strategic Marketing Planning: Problems and Analytical Approaches*. Upper Saddle River NJ: Prentice Hall.

Armstrong, J.S. (1982) 'The value of formal planning for strategic decisions'. *Strategic Management Journal* 3(3), 197–211.

Hill, T. and Westbrook, R. (1997) 'SWOT analysis: It's time for a product recall'. *Long Range Planning* 30(1), 46–52.

Menon, A., Bharadwaj S.G., Adidam, P.T. and Edison, S.W. (1999) 'Antecedents and consequences of marketing strategy making. A model and a test'. *Journal of Marketing* 63(2), 18–40.

Weihrich, H. (1982) 'The TOWS matrix – A tool for situational analysis'. *Long Range Planning* 15(2), 54–66.

part

two

Organisation and governance

5

Balanced scorecard

■ **Why use it?** The balanced scorecard helps to clarify the organisation's long-term vision, goals and objectives in terms of key performance indicators and to monitor the organisation's performance and progress.

■ **What does it do?** The balanced scorecard is a top-down method for defining an organisation's goals and objectives and monitoring progress. It comprises four different perspectives in which progress is monitored. For each perspective, relevant key performance indicators are identified, based on the organisation's mission and vision.

■ **When to use it?** The BSC can be used as an alternative to traditional financial accounting methods. It not only measures an organisation's performance from a financial and commercial perspective, but also monitors progress from internal business processes and an organisational learning perspective.

■ **What questions will it help you answer?** How can I articulate and communicate my strategy, and align individual organisational and cross-departmental initiatives to achieve a common goal by focussing on a balanced set of key performance indicators which are recognisable throughout the organisation, and which will lead ultimately to substantial and lasting performance improvement?

The big picture

The balanced scorecard (BSC) was developed by Kaplan and Norton in 1992 as an alternative to traditional performance measurement approaches that focus solely on financial indicators, and are based purely on a company's past performance. The BSC is a top-down method for defining an organisation's goals and objectives (Figure 5.1). It comprises four different perspectives in which progress is monitored. For each perspective, relevant key performance indicators are identified, based on the organisation's mission and vision. These help to clarify the organisation's long-term vision. In this way, an organisation is able to monitor its goals, strategy and objectives, and make any necessary corrective measures promptly.

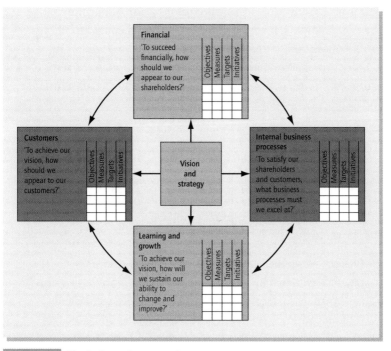

Figure 5.1 The balanced scorecard

When to use it

The BSC can be used as an alternative to traditional financial accounting methods. It measures a company's performance across four perspectives: *financial, internal business processes, learning and growth* and *customers*. Financial measures are complemented by non-financial measures that drive long-term financial success, by asking questions such as:

- What is important for our shareholders?
- How do customers perceive us?
- Which internal processes can add value?
- Are we innovative and ready for the future?

The BSC monitors not only past performance, but also present performance and tries to capture information about how well the organisation is positioned for the future. It is used to monitor organisational performance transparently and via multiple measures. It enables management to take appropriate corrective action when necessary, which will lead ultimately to substantial and lasting performance improvement.

How to use it

To create a BSC, a company first has to define its mission and vision, as these determine the desired performance and thus the success factors and key performance indicators for the four different perspectives:

- **Financial perspective.** Managers need timely and accurate financial data to manage their business. Important indicators are return on investment (ROI) and value added (economic value added). However, other measures can be added depending on the characteristics of the company and the industry in which it operates.

- **Customer perspective.** Customer service and satisfaction are viewed as important issues for all organisations, as poor customer performance ultimately leads to a company's decline: dissatisfied customers will find other suppliers to fulfil their needs! Measuring satisfaction, retention, market and account share provides an insight into how customers perceive the company. Possible indicators include customer profitability, return policy, handling service calls, market share in target segments, and claims and complaints handling.

- **Internal process.** Information on the performance of the company's operational activities helps to monitor and steer the effectiveness of the organisation's activities. Indicators on internal processes give management an insight into the effectiveness of their operations. Quality, response and cycle time, costs, new product development, time to market, but also break-even time realised, and new sales as a percentage of total sales are indicators for measuring the performance of a company's operation.

- **Learning and growth.** Indicators for the learning and growth perspective provide an insight into the successfulness of human resources management and knowledge, and innovation management. Important indicators in this perspective are employee satisfaction, staff retention rate, revenue/value added per employee, strategic redundancy in job skills, new ideas per employee and information availability relative to need.

Do's

- Use the BSC to articulate your strategy, to communicate your strategy and to help align individual, organisational and cross-departmental initiatives to achieve a common goal.
- Refresh the BSC as often as needed, so that you can focus on and monitor the right goals.

> **Don'ts**
>
> ■ The BSC is not a tool for controlling behaviour or evaluating past performance.

The final analysis

There is nothing new about the call for measuring non-financial indicators, but Kaplan and Norton (1992) have to receive the credit for advocating the impact of balanced measures from different perspectives. A CEO is still likely to be biased towards financial measures. The BSC forces a company to focus on a balanced set of key performance indicators which are recognisable throughout the organisation and which will lead ultimately to substantial and lasting performance improvement.

However, it is not easy to find a correctly balanced set of performance indicators. Note that an appropriate number of indicators in a BSC for top management is 12–16 if there is full consensus in a company's management team regarding these indicators. In addition, the main indicators have to be broken down into underlying indicators that can be acted upon by middle and lower management. Otherwise, there is a risk that employees will focus only on the few overall goals on the scorecard.

Finally, the BSC has to be updated regularly, depending on the type of business, to prevent the wrong measures being carried out.

References

Kaplan, R. and Norton, D. (1992) 'The Balanced Scorecard: Measures that drive performance'. *Harvard Business Review* Jan–Feb, 70(1), 71–80.

Kaplan, R. and Norton, D. (1996) *The Balanced Scorecard: Translating Strategy into Action*. Cambridge MA: Harvard Business School Press.

6

Benchmarking

- **Why use it?** Benchmarking is about comparing the organisation to the average of the benchmark population. This gives companies insight into their own relative situation and how the organisation performs compared to the average.

- **What does it do?** Benchmarking can provide comparative data that may prompt management to improve performance. Benchmarking will identify the gap between the best practices and the present performance of the organisation in order to create new standards and/or improve processes.

- **When to use it?** Benchmarking can be used to improve performance and learn from competitors, enabling an organisation to become better than its competitors or set new standards in the industry.

- **What questions will it help you answer?** How good are we at what we do? Are we as good as others at what we do? Is the grass really greener on the other side?

The big picture

Benchmarking is the systematic comparison of organisational processes and performances based on predefined indicators. The objective of benchmarking is to find the gap between the best practices and the present performance of the organisation in order to create new standards and/or improve processes.

There are five basic types of benchmarking:

1 **The historical benchmark** – a comparison of the indicators and performances of the organisation with its performance at a previous moment in time.

2 **The internal benchmark** – a comparison of performance and practices between parts of an organisation, e.g. between business units.

3 **The competitive benchmark** – a comparison of the indicators and performances of an organisation with those of its direct competitors.

4 **The functional benchmark** – a comparison of the indicators and performances of an organisation and those of a number of organisations within the broader range of the industry.

5 **The generic benchmark** – a comparison of the indicators and performances of an organisation with those of organisations from unrelated industries to find overall best practices.

All types of benchmark can be helpful: they give an organisation an insight into its strengths and weaknesses; they are objective; they uncover problems and indicate possible improvements; and they point out norms, new guidelines and fresh ideas to improve an organisation's performance.

Different methods for benchmarking vary to the extent that they include situational characteristics and/or explanatory factors to account for differences between organisations (Figure 6.1). Moreover, some benchmarking methods include prospective

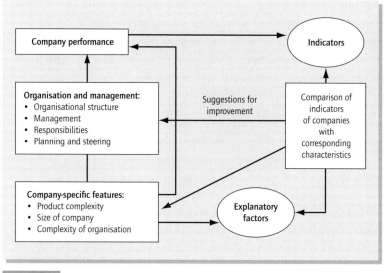

Figure 6.1 Benchmarking

trends and developments of best practices, or other practical issues that may arise in an industry.

When to use it

The use of benchmarking depends on the goal. Bearing in mind the difference between intention and action, we can define the objective of benchmarking as the provision of an answer to any one of the following questions:

- How good are we at what we do?
- Are we as good as others at what we do?
- If the grass is really greener on the neighbours' lawn, how did they do that?

Usually, benchmarking is about comparing the organisation against the average of the benchmark population. This gives companies an insight into their own situation and into how the organisation performs compared with the average. Often, however, it is even more ambitious for the organisation to compare itself not against the average but against the best, or, for example, the top 25 per cent. By coupling this comparison to certain good or best practices, it often becomes very clear in which areas improvement actions are relevant.

The scope of a benchmarking project is determined by the impact it may have on the organisation; by the degree to which the results can be communicated freely, in order to increase the success rate of corresponding improvement projects; and by the level of effort required to achieve results that are valuable in practice.

However, benchmarking does not lead to answers regarding how to improve, and it usually can't give declarations of differences in performance, but rather gives insights into what to improve. Benchmarks offer no judgment and only when there is no explanation for a deviation does it make sense to look for improvements (e.g. relatively high training costs can be the result of a certain strategic choice that has to do with investing in employee skills).

How to use it

Benchmarking juxtaposes existing information. Good benchmarking is often trickier than it appears at first sight. First, there should be very clear and unambiguous definitions. Then, measurement methods that objectively and properly measure what the organisation wants to compare are to be defined. When measuring at the organisation itself is already difficult, measuring at other organisations is likely to be even more so, if not impossible. Besides, organisations in general are often reluctant to disclose information to a competitor, even when the outcomes of the benchmark are made available to all participants. So many organisations make use of (independent) benchmark databases.

Next, the organisations (or peers) that are used in benchmarking should be selected. Ideally they would perform better than, or at least equally as well as, the target organisation (or peers), as this brings most lessons to improve the organisation. In general, peers are identified via industry experts and publications. However, differences in products, processes, structure or the type of leadership and management style make it difficult to make direct comparisons between organisations. It is possible to overcome this difficulty in a practical way. Assumptions about the performance of the target firm can be made more accurate by benchmarking the indicator (e.g. 'delivery reliability') according to a number of explanatory factors. It is possible to compare organisations in cross-section for some indicators, based on explanatory factors. Reliable delivery of a product, for instance, depends on the complexity of the product. Therefore, a group of firms that have a similar level of product complexity will have similar indicators and will be a suitable peer group for benchmarking reliable delivery performance (see Figure 6.2).

After carrying out the benchmark, reporting on comparative performance per participant is done and improvement directions for deviations are defined per participant.

Benchmarking entails the following (sometimes overlapping) steps:

1 Determine the scope of the project.

2 Choose the benchmark partner(s).

3 Determine measure(s), units, indicators and the data collection method.

4 Collect the data.

5 Analyse discrepancies – get to the facts behind the numbers.

6 Present the analysis and discuss implications in terms of (new) goals.

7 Generate an action plan and/or procedures.

8 Monitor progress by continuously performing a benchmark.

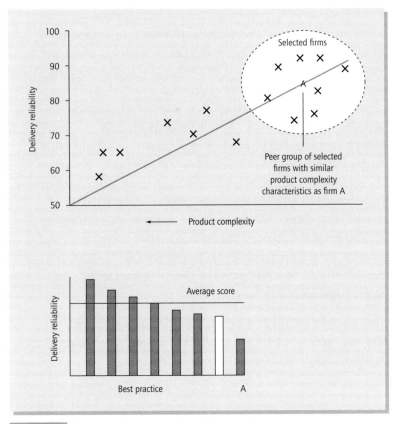

Figure 6.2 Example of benchmarking: (a) selecting a peer group; (b) finding best practice

The final analysis

Benchmarking is not straightforward. Too often, semi-committed managers or consultants perform benchmarking without the use of predetermined measurements or the proper tools for detailed analysis and presentation. Undoubtedly, many benchmarking projects end in dismay; an exercise often justifiably portrayed as being as futile as comparing apples and pears. Even when performed in a structured way, the 'we are different to them' syndrome prevents benchmarking from leading to changes for the better. Furthermore, competitive sensitivity can stifle the free flow of information, even inside an organisation.

By applying explanatory factors, benchmarking can not only provide comparative data that may prompt management to improve performance (indeed, it highlights improvement opportunities), but it also indicates original, but proven, solutions to apparently difficult problems. We therefore argue that it is precisely the differences between the firms in the peer group that should be encouraged, rather than trying to exclude organisations because of so-called 'non-comparable' products or processes.

A word of warning however: becoming as good as the benchmark (i.e. the average of the benchmark-population) should never be a goal in itself: no organisation will beat competition by being only equally as good!

Reference

Watson, G.H. (1993) *Strategic Benchmarking: How to Rate your Company's Performance Against the World's Best*. New York: John Wiley & Sons.

7

The value chain

- **Why use it?** The value chain model can provide helpful insights into the effectiveness of the chain of activities that deliver the organisation's product or service. The model divides the generic value-adding activities of an organisation into primary and secondary activities. An advantage or disadvantage may be identified within any of the activities detailed.

- **What does it do?** In order to analyse a company's competitive advantage (or lack of one), the value chain can be used to look in detail at the company's (discrete) activities. Once the firm's activities have been broken down to a sufficient level of detail, the relative performance of each can be analysed.

- **When to use it?** The model can be used to analyse the performance of the organisation's activities and to develop competitive advantage(s). By identifying the potential value to the company of separate activities, a firm can gain insight into how to maximise value creation whilst minimising costs, and hence create a competitive advantage.

■ **What questions will it help you answer?** What value does each activity that my organisation undertakes add? What is the total combined value of all these activities in relation to the cost of providing the product or service?

The big picture

According to Porter (1985), competitive advantage can only be understood by looking at the firm as a whole. Cost advantages and successful differentiation are found by considering the chain of activities a firm performs to deliver value to its customers. The value chain model divides the generic value-adding activities of an organisation into primary and secondary activities. An advantage or disadvantage can occur within any of the five primary or four secondary activities. Together, these activities constitute the value chain of any firm (Figure 7.1).

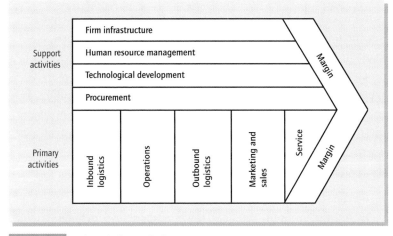

Figure 7.1 Value chain analysis

Source: after *Competitive Advantage: Creating and Sustaining Superior Performance*, Free Press (Porter, M.E. 1985), Copyright © 1985, 1998 by Michael E. Porter, all rights reserved. Reproduced with the permission of Simon & Schuster Publishing Group, a Division of Simon and Schuster, Inc.

When to use it

The model can be used to examine the development of competitive advantage. By identifying the potential value to the company of separate activities, a firm can gain insight into how to maximise value creation whilst minimising costs, and hence create a competitive advantage.

The value chain is also useful for outsourcing and offshoring decisions. A better understanding of the links between activities can lead to better make-or-buy decisions which can result in either a cost or a differentiation advantage.

How to use it

In order to analyse the competitive advantage (or lack of one), Porter suggests using the value chain to separate the company's activities therein into detailed discrete activities. The relative performance of the company can be determined once the firm's activities have been broken down to a sufficient level of detail.

Porter has identified a set of generic activities. The primary activities include inbound logistics, operations, outbound logistics, marketing and sales, and services. The support activities include procurement, technology development, human resource management and the firm's infrastructure. Each activity should be analysed for its added value. Also the total combined value of all these activities when considered in relation to the costs of providing the product or service has to be analysed, as this will dictate the level (or lack of) profit margin:

- **Inbound logistics** – activities include receiving, storing, listing and grouping inputs to the product. It also includes functions such as materials handling, warehousing, inventory management, transportation scheduling and managing suppliers.

- **Operations** – include machining, packaging, assembly, maintenance of equipment, testing and operational management.

- **Outbound logistics** – refers to activities such as order processing, warehousing, scheduling transportation and distribution management.

■ **Marketing and sales** – includes all activities that make or convince buyers to purchase the company's products, e.g. advertising, promotion, selling, pricing, channel selection and retail management.

■ **Service** – is concerned with maintaining the product after sale, thus guaranteeing quality and/or adding value in other ways, such as installation, training, servicing, providing spare parts and upgrading. Service enhances the product value and allows for after-sale (commercial) interaction with the buyer.

■ **Procurement** – is referred to by Porter as a secondary activity, although many purchasing gurus would argue that it is (at least partly) a primary activity. Included are activities such as purchasing raw materials, servicing, supplies, negotiating contracts with suppliers and securing building leases.

■ **Technology development** – Porter refers to activities such as R&D, product and/or process improvements, (re)design and developing new services.

■ **Human resource management** – includes recruitment and education, as well as compensation, employee retention and other means of capitalising on human resources.

■ **Infrastructure** – such as general management, planning procedures, finance, accounting, public affairs and quality management – can make the difference between success and (despite the best intentions in the world) failure.

The final analysis

Since Porter introduced the value chain model in the mid-1980s, strategic planners and consultants have used it extensively to map out a company's strengths and shortcomings (see Figure 7.2). When strategic alliances and merger and acquisition (M&A) deals are analysed, the value chain is used frequently to gain a quick

There are various ways in which we have seen consultants use the value chain:

A visualisation of the company or a competitor

The company

A quick and dirty identification of (lack of) strengths

+ direct logistics system
+ dedicated sales force etc.

Comparison of competitive strengths

versus

Analysis to establish potential match for M&A or strategic alliances

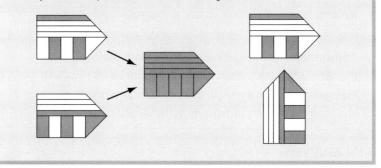

Figure 7.2 **The value chain: a versatile tool for consultants**

Source: based on Porter (1985)

overview of a possible match. For example, if one company is strong in logistics, and the other in sales and service, together they would make an agile, highly commercial competitor.

There is one downside: it is difficult to measure or rate competitive strengths objectively. Especially when trying to map the entire value chain and apply quantitative measurements or ratings, many companies find themselves employing large numbers of strategic analysts, planners and consultants.

The term value grid has recently been introduced. This term highlights the fact that competition in the value chain has been shifting away from the strict view defined by the traditional value chain model (Pil & Holweg, 2006).

References

Pil, F.K. and Holweg, M. (2006) 'Evolving from value chain to value grid'. *MIT Sloan Management Review* 47(4), 72–79.

Porter, M.E. (1985) *Competitive Advantage: Creating and Sustaining Superior Performance.* New York: Free Press.

part
three

Finance

8

Activity-based costing

- **Why use it?** Activity-based costing is used to allocate all costs to the activities the costs are incurred for.

- **What does it do?** Contrary to traditional cost accounting methods, activity-based costing (ABC) calculates the 'true' costs of products, customers or services by attributing direct and indirect costs based, not on volume, but on actual time and resources spent on required activities.

- **When to use it?** Activity-based costing can be useful if products/services or customer groups vary in complexity and handling costs.

- **What questions will it help you answer?** How can I determine customer value accurately, considering all costs I incur for this customer? What (indirect) costs are too high per activity? Are there any costly products that I should charge more for?

The big picture

Activity-based costing is a cost accounting model. It is used to allocate all costs, based on time spent on activities relating to products and services provided for customers. Traditional cost accounting models allocate indirect costs (overheads) based on volume. As a result, the costs of high-volume products tend to be over-rated, whereas the costs of low-volume products are under-rated. Contrary to traditional cost accounting methods, activity-based costing (ABC) calculates the 'true' costs of products, customers or services by attributing indirect costs based, not on volume, but on required or performed activities.

Instead of using broad arbitrary percentages to allocate costs, ABC seeks to identify cause-and-effect relationships to assign costs objectively. Once the costs of the activities have been identified, the cost of each activity is attributed to each product, to the extent that the product uses the activity. In this way, ABC often identifies areas of high overhead costs per unit and is able to direct attention towards finding ways to reduce the costs or to charging more for costly products.

There is an underlying assumption when using the ABC model that costs are generated not by the products or customers themselves, but by the activities required to make or serve them. As different products require different activities, each of which uses a different level of resources, the allocation of costs should be weighted accordingly.

When making business decisions, knowledge of true costs can help to (Figure 8.1):

■ establish economic break-even points;

■ identify 'profit makers' and 'losers' (i.e. assess 'customer value');

■ highlight opportunities for improvement;

■ compare investment alternatives.

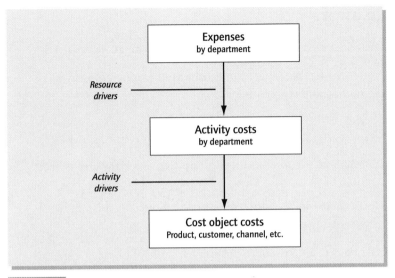

Figure 8.1 Activity-based costing

When to use it

Activity-based costing can be useful if the overhead is high and the products/customers are highly varied regarding complexity and handling costs. Activity-based costing turns indirect costs into direct costs. A more accurate cost management system than traditional cost accounting, ABC identifies opportunities for improving the effectiveness and efficiency of business processes by determining the 'true' cost of a product or service.

Other models that are similar to ABC are total cost of ownership (TCO) and life cycle costs. TCO is a calculation that reflects the total cost of the investment, including one-time purchases, recurring costs and operating costs. The TCO concept is widely used in information technology (IT) implementations where the benefits are hard to quantify and the focus is on minimising the project costs. A life cycle cost analysis calculates the cost of a system or product during its entire life span.

How to use it

There are five steps involved in performing a simple ABC analysis:

1   Define the cost objects, indirect activities and resources used for the indirect activities.

2   Determine the costs per indirect activity.

3   Identify the cost drivers for each resource.

4   Calculate the total indirect product costs for the cost object type.

5   Divide the total costs by quantity for indirect cost per individual cost object.

Cost objects are products, customers, services or anything else that is the object of the cost-accounting endeavour. Activities could be anything a company does to operate its business: receiving, loading, packing, handling, calling, explaining, selling, buying, promoting, calculating/computing, writing orders, reading orders, etc. Indirect activities are not directly attributable to cost objects. Resources are machines, computers, people or any other capacity or asset that can be (partly) allocated to an activity.

The final analysis

Activity-based costing enables segmentation based on true profitability and helps to determine customer value more accurately. As such, it is the first step towards activity-based management (ABM). ABC does not assess efficiency or the productivity of activities, even though this may be extremely important for improvement. In addition, ABC assumes that it is possible to identify unique cost objects, activities and resources. At the end of the day, the outcome of an ABC analysis is only as accurate as its input.

Reference

Kaplan, R.S. and Cooper, R. (1998) *Cost and Effect: Using Integrated Cost Systems to Drive Profitability and Performance*. Cambridge MA: Harvard Business School Press.

Discounted cash flow (DCF) and net present value (NPV)

- **Why use it?** Discounted cash flow is a method to assess and compare the current and future value of an asset. Discounted cash flows (DCF) are calculated to assess the future cash flows that could come from an investment opportunity.

- **What does it do?** The DCF method is an approach to valuation, whereby projected future cash flows are discounted at an interest rate that reflects the perceived risk of the cash flows. The interest rate is reflected by the time value of money (investors could have invested in other opportunities), and a risk premium.

- **When to use it?** DCF (and NPV) is used for capital budgeting or investment decisions.

- **What questions will it help you answer?** Which investment projects should my organisation accept? What is the total amount of capital expenditure of my organisation?

The big picture

Discounted cash flow (DCF) is a method to assess and compare the current and future values of an asset. DCFs are calculated to assess the future cash flows that could come from an investment opportunity. A DCF analysis is a valuation method used to estimate the attractiveness of an investment opportunity. The total incremental stream of future cash flows from a capital project is tested to assess the return it delivers to the investor. If this return exceeds the required, or hurdle, rate, the project is recommended on financial terms, and vice versa. The DCF analysis discounts the future cash flows to their present-day value. Using future free cash flow projections and discounting them to a present value, the potential for investment can be evaluated. If the value arrived at is higher than the current cost of the investment, the opportunity may be a good one. DCF also converts future earnings into today's money. Often these analyses are called net present value (NPV) calculations: determining today's (present) value of tomorrow's earnings (Figure 9.1).

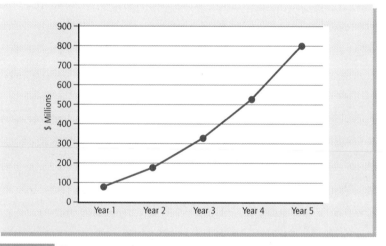

Figure 9.1   Net present value

When to use it

Discounted cash flow (and NPV) is used for capital budgeting or investment decisions to determine:

▪ which investment projects a firm should accept;

▪ the total amount of capital expenditure;

▪ how a portfolio of projects should be financed.

A relevant cost is an expected future cost that will differ from alternatives. The DCF method is an approach to valuation, whereby projected future cash flows are discounted at an interest rate that reflects the perceived risk of the cash flows. The interest rate reflects the time value of money (investors could have invested in other opportunities), and a risk premium.

How to use it

The discounted cash flow can be calculated by projecting all future cash flows and making a calculated assumption on what the current value of that future cash flow is according to the following formula:

$$\sum_{1}^{n} \frac{\text{Future cash flows}}{(1 + \text{discount rate})^n}$$

The discount rate can be determined based on the risk-free rate plus a risk premium. Based on the economic principle that money loses value over time (time value of money), meaning that every investor would prefer to receive their money today rather than tomorrow, a small premium is incorporated in the discount rate to give investors a small compensation for receiving their money not now, but in the future. This premium is the so-called risk-free rate.

Next, a small compensation is incorporated against the risk that future cash flows may not eventually materialise, and that the investors will therefore not receive their money at all. This second compensation is the risk premium and it should reflect the so-called opportunity costs of the investors.

These two compensating factors, the risk-free rate and the risk premium, together determine the discount rate. With this discount rate, the future cash flow can be discounted to the present value. Based on the future cash flows and their present-day value, the DCF analysis can be used as basis for an NPV analysis. This NPV of a project or investment proposal can then be compared with other projects and proposals, allowing an investment decision to be made. A calculation example is presented in the following box:

Time	t	t + 1	t + 2	t + 3	t + 4 … n
Investment	215.000	25.000	25.000		
Cash flows		2.000	4.000	4.000	5.000
Total cash flow	215.000	23.000	21.000	4.000	5.000
Discount rate = 10%					
Discount rate $(1 / (1 + 10\%)^n)$	0	0.91	0.83	0.75	0.68
Net Present Value (NPV)	15.000–	2.727–	826–	3.005	34.151
NPV total	18.602				

The final analysis

First published in 1938 by John Burr Williams in a paper based on his PhD, 'Discounted cash flow statements', DCF analysis and NPV methods have become common all over the world.

DCF models are powerful, but they have their faults. DCF is merely a mechanical valuation tool, which makes it subject to the axiom 'garbage in, garbage out'. Small changes in inputs can result in large changes in the value of a company. The discount rate is especially difficult to calculate. Future cash flows are also hard to forecast, especially if the largest part of the future cash inflows is received after 5 or 10 years. Also the discount rate and, more particularly, the risk premium are sometimes difficult to calculate objectively. Alternative calculation methods have more sophisticated approaches to assess the expected return for investors.

References

Brealey, R.A. and Myers, S.C. (2003) *Principles of Corporate Finance*, 7th edn. London: McGraw-Hill.

Walsh, C. (2008) *Key Management Ratios: The 100+ Ratios Every Manager Needs to Know*. Harlow: Pearson.

Willams, J.B. (1938) *Theory of Investment Value*. Cambridge: Harvard University Press.

part

four

Marketing and sales

10

4Ps of marketing (Kotler)

- **Why use it?** Kotler's marketing mix is a tactical toolkit that an organisation can use to state and execute its marketing strategy. As an organisation can adjust the '4Ps' categories on a regular basis, it is able to keep pace with the changing needs of customers in a specific market segment.

- **What does it do?** When grouped into the categories product, price, place and promotion, marketing decisions can be justified and chosen deliberately.

- **When to use it?** An analysis of the elements that form the marketing mix of an organisation, the 4Ps introduced by Philip Kotler, can give a company insights into their current and potential interactions with current and potential customers and the position they occupy in the perception of its customers.

■ **What questions will it help you answer?** Do you actually produce what your customers want? Are your products available in the right quantities, in the right place, at the right time, at the right price and in the right conditions? How can you best inform/educate groups of customers about your organisation and its products?

The big picture

Philip Kotler introduced what is commonly known as the 4Ps of marketing: product, price, place and promotion. The '4Ps', or the marketing mix, is a description of the strategic position of a product in the marketplace. The premise of the model is that marketing decisions generally fall into the following four controllable categories:

- Product (characteristics)
- Price
- Place (distribution)
- Promotion.

When grouped into these four categories, marketing decisions can be justified and chosen deliberately, taking into account the intended effects (Figure 10.1).

When to use it

Marketing (and sales) is the functional field in any organisation that bridges the customers' perspective with the organisational perspective. An analysis of the elements that form the marketing mix of an organisation, the 4Ps introduced by Philip Kotler, gives insights into the company's current and potential interactions with current and potential customers and the position the company has in the perception of its customers. The marketing mix is a tactical toolkit that an organisation can use as an integral part of its marketing strategy to realise its corporate strategy. As an organisation can adjust the 4Ps categories on a regular basis, it is able to keep pace with the changing needs of customers in a specific market segment.

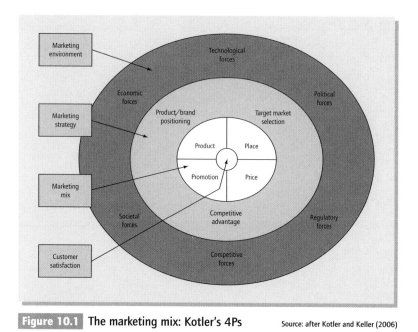

Figure 10.1 The marketing mix: Kotler's 4Ps   Source: after Kotler and Keller (2006)

How to use it

There are three basic steps:

1 **Step 1: Research.** In order to develop a marketing mix that precisely matches the needs of the customers in the target market, an organisation first has to gather information on each of the 4Ps.

2 **Step 2: Analyse the variables and determine the optimum mix.** Next an assessment is to be made as to whether the 4Ps are well enough aligned to each other. An optimal marketing mix has to be determined, which will allow the organisation to strike a balance between satisfying its customers and maximising the organisation's profitability. This means making decisions regarding the issues in each of the categories illustrated in the following table.

Product decisions	Price decisions	Distribution (place) decisions	Promotion decisions
Brand name	Pricing strategy (skim, and penetration)	Distribution channels	Promotional strategy (push or pull)
Functionality styling		Market coverage (inclusive, selective or exclusive distribution)	Advertising
Quality	Suggested retail price		Personal selling and sales force
Safety		Specific channel members	
Packaging	Volume discounts and wholesale pricing		Sales promotions
Repairs and support		Inventory management	Public relations and publicity
Warranty	Cash and early payment discounts		Marketing
Accessories and services		Warehousing	Communications budget
	Seasonal pricing	Distribution centres	
	Bundling	Order processing	
	Price flexibility	Transportation	
	Price discrimination	Reverse logistics	

- **Product** – Do you actually produce what your customers want? Possible decisions and activities regarding the product include: new product development; modification of existing products; and elimination of products that are no longer attractive, or that are unprofitable. There is also a variety of activities closely linked to the product that can be considered, such as branding, packaging, guarantees and the handling of complaints.

- **Place (distribution)** – Are your products available in the right quantities, in the right place, at the right time? Can you achieve this whilst keeping inventory, transport and storage costs as low as possible? Analyse and compare the various distribution possibilities, after which the most appropriate option can be selected. Again, there are a number of activities related to this category, such as selecting and motivating intermediaries; controlling inventory and managing transport; and storing as efficiently as possible.

- **Promotion** – How can you best inform/educate groups of customers about your organisation and its products? Different types of promotional activities may be necessary, depending on whether the organisation wishes to launch a new product, to increase awareness with regard to special features of an existing one, or to retain interest in a product that has been available in the same form for a long time. Therefore, decisions must be taken as to the most effective way of delivering the desired message to the target group.

- **Price** – How much are your customers willing to pay? The value obtained in an exchange is critical to consumers, in addition to which price is often used as a competitive tool, not only in price wars, but also for image enhancement. Pricing decisions are thus highly sensitive.

3 **Step 3: Check.** Monitoring and control on an ongoing basis are essential to ascertain the effectiveness of the chosen mix and how well it is being executed.

The final analysis

Over the years, the 4Ps have become an institution. But one of the main problems with the 4Ps is that they have a tendency to keep increasing in number, prompting the question 'Where does marketing stop?' Of all the candidates, the 'people' factor is undoubtedly the most widely accepted 'fifth P'. After all, people manipulate the marketing mix as marketers; they make products/ services available to marketplace as intermediaries; they create the need for marketing as consumers/buyers; they play an important role when it comes to service levels, recruitment, training, retention, and so on.

It is tempting to view the marketing mix variables as controllable, but remember that there are limits: price changes may be restricted by economic conditions or government regulations; changes in design and promotion are expensive and cannot be effected overnight; and people are expensive to hire and train. Do not forget to keep an eye on what is happening in the outside world, as some events may have a greater impact than you think.

Ultimately, successful marketing is a matter of gut feeling and acting on hunches. Whilst the marketing mix is a useful instrument when it comes to analysing and ordering, the multitude of marketing decisions has to be considered.

References

Kotler, P. and Armstrong, G. (2011) *Marketing Management*, 14th edn. Upper Saddle River NJ: Prentice-Hall.

Kotler, P. and Keller, K.L. (2000) *A Framework for Marketing Management*, 3rd edn. Upper Saddle River NJ: Prentice-Hall.

Kotler, P. and Keller, K.L. (2006) *Marketing Management: Analysis, Planning, Implementation and Control*, 12th edn. Upper Saddle River NJ: Pearson Education.

chapter

11

Customer journey mapping

- **Why use it?** Customer journey mapping is a
  model used to map out all interactions between
  customers and the organisation from the
  perspective of the customer, with the intention of
  improving these interactions and thus increasing
  sales and customer satisfaction.

- **What does it do?** Customer journey mapping
  is a way of seeing things from the customer's
  point of view. It's not about just describing their
  experience, but also examining how they feel
  about what happens to them and analysing
  what the company can do better to improve the
  customer experience.

- **When to use it?** Customer journey mapping is
  a model for gaining greater customer insight. It
  can be used as part of a business improvement
  process, or as part of a design or restructuring
  process to plan out the perfect customer journey
  (or at least the best achievable one). It can also be
  used when training customer-facing teams to help

improve empathy with customers or to identify where attention and investment is required to improve the customer experience. It can also be used to provide input for the company's strategy: by analysing the mapped-out customer experience and customer feedback, additional future business opportunities might be found.

▤ **What question will it help you answer?** How can I increase customer satisfaction (and thus sales)?

The big picture

Customer journey mapping is a model for mapping all interactions between customers and the organisation from the perspective of the customer, with the intention of improving these interactions and, by doing so, increasing sales and customer satisfaction. Although the model has been around since the late 1980s, with the rise of online customer interactions (social media, e-commerce, etc.) customer journey mapping is used by many companies to optimise activities and interactions both offline and online, and to align between both channels.

Customer journey mapping is a way of seeing things from the customers' point of view. It is not about just describing their experience, but also how they feel about what happens to them and then analysing what the company can do better to improve this experience.

When to use it

Customer journey mapping is a model for gaining greater customer insight. It can be used as part of a business improvement process – with potential for both improving the customer experience and reducing the costs of providing a service. It can also be used as part of a design or restructuring process, drawing up the perfect customer journey – or at least the best achievable one. Moreover, it can be used as part of training and insight material to help customer-facing teams improve their empathy with customers or to identify where attention and investment are required to improve customer experience – or where savings can be made while not harming customer satisfaction.

Another application of customer journey mapping is as a tool for providing input for the company's strategy: based on the mapped-out customer experiences and customer feedback, additional future business opportunities might be found.

Key steps	1 Recognise need	2 Become aware of products	3 Orientate	4 Decide	5 Purchase	6 Use	7 Repeat purchase
Key activities of organisation							
Key customer actions							
Emotional experience ☺ ☹							
Perceived barriers							
Suggestions and improvements							
Optimisation potential							

Figure 11.1 Customer journey mapping

How to use it

Customer journey mapping is all about the customer and his/
her experiences with the company (see Figure 11.1). This requires
essential knowledge of customers, so it is imperative that
those involved in mapping the customer journey should have
first-hand experience with customer interaction. In addition, customer satisfaction surveys are valuable input.

Customer journey mapping starts with analysing the interaction
of customers with the organisation. Often this interaction is split
into key steps. For each step, the activities of the organisation and
the activities the customer has to perform are identified. And for
each step – and each activity – the emotional experience for the
customer should be assessed. This emotional experience is key to
customer journey mapping and the starting point for identifying
improvement potential in the company's interaction with customers. When there is a negative emotion from the customer, one
should look into the activities performed by the organisation. Are
they up to standard? Do they meet the customer expectations?
And one should also look into the activities performed by the
customer. Do they match the customer expectations (and value-
for-money perceptions)? Are they facilitated by the organisation
in any way, or the right way? When there is a positive emotion,
analysis is also useful to see if further improvement is possible, to
learn how this positive emotion might be realised in other steps
and activities, and to learn what causes this positive emotion to
lessen (or further increase) in the next step(s) and how that experience can be transferred to other steps. The latter is, of course,
also very important when trying to increase conversion rates (i.e.
increase the number of potential customers who become actual
customers).

Customer journey mapping finishes by identifying suggestions
for improvement of each step, with the aim of increasing customer satisfaction (and thus sales).

Customer journey mapping benefits from being visualised. In this visualisation, the key steps in the interaction (from the customers' perspective) should be leading. When drawing up a customer journey map for business improvement, it might involve the following elements (see also Figure 11.1):

- Key journey steps – all the steps customers go through in chronological order.

- Actions and activities from the organisation in each step.

- Actions and activities to be performed by the customer in each step. Often the interactions between the customer and the company are specifically highlighted and referred to as touchpoints. These touchpoints are where activities by the organisation meet and overlap with activities by the customer: this is when interaction occurs. However, touchpoints do not have to appear in every step.

- The emotional experience of customers (their thoughts and feelings) at each step, with a graphical representation of customers' emotional state and their satisfaction levels at each step of the process (often called a 'customer experience chart' or 'heartbeat chart').

- The barriers (as perceived by the customer) to moving forward to the next step – structural, process, cost, implementation or other barriers.

- Improvements and suggestions that would increase customer satisfaction in each step, and/or improvements and suggestions that would ease customer transition to the next step.

- Assessment of potential savings by optimising inefficient, combining (partially) overlapping and/or leaving out unnecessary activities in steps or even complete steps.

The final analysis

One of the strengths of customer journey mapping is that it helps to improve customer experiences in both offline and online interactions with the company. And it allows assessment of processes involving both tangible products and intangible service delivery. Another strong point is that it aims at both optimising the customer's experience (more sales) and the efficiency of the company's activities (less costs, more margin).

The model is scalable: it can be used both within a sales team meeting and at board level with extensive customer surveys. In both cases, it is likely that improvements will be found.

The visualisation of the 'customer journey' and the customer experiences is one of the reasons the model has seen increased popularity (especially in e-commerce). The visualisation is not necessarily linear, but could also take the shape of a 'wheel' with sequential steps in customer interaction. This shape also allows continued and replacement purchases to be linked up (as the 'after-sales step' and 'pre-purchase orientation step' connect in the wheel). Such a round, wheel-like shape is also called as a customer activity cycle, with Lego's customer experience wheel being a well-known example.

References

Liedtka, J., Ogilvie, T. and Brazonske, R. (2013) *The Designing for Growth Field Book: A Step-By-Step Project Guide*. New York: Columbia Business School Publishing.

Richardson, A. (2010) 'Using customer journey maps to improve customer experience'. *HBR Blog Network* (posted 15 November 2010). http://blogs.hbr.org/2010/11/using-customer-journey-maps-to/.

Shostack, G.L. (1984) 'Design services that deliver'. *Harvard Business Review* (84115), 133–139.

12

Stakeholder management

■ **Why use it?** Stakeholder management helps to identify the interests of groups and individuals that are important to the company and this in turn helps determine how to act upon them.

■ **What does it do?** Stakeholder management consists of a set of tools to assess stakeholders and to analyse their interests and their relation with the organisation. Most important in this is the assessment of the power of the stakeholder.

■ **When to use it?** With stakeholder management, a company can form an idea of: who the most important (dominant) stakeholders are, how stakeholders relate to each other, how the various stakeholders move in their relationship with the company, what influencing power the stakeholders (should) have on the company and how the company could (and/or should) act on behalf of a stakeholder.

■ **What question will it help you answer?** What resistance is there to (proposed) decisions and changes among stakeholders and how can I convince any (internal or external) opponents thus creating support?

The big picture

Every company interacts with its environment and therefore has to deal with individuals, groups, companies and other organisations: the stakeholders. Some of these relationships are intentional and desirable, while others are not. All have in common the fact that they are involved with the organisation in a certain way and thus have an interest in the activities and objectives of the organisation. Stakeholder management helps to identify the interests of groups and individuals that are important to the company and then to act upon them. It consists of a set of tools to assess stakeholders and to analyse their interests and their relationship with the organisation. The most important factor in this is the assessment of the power of the stakeholder (Figure 12.1).

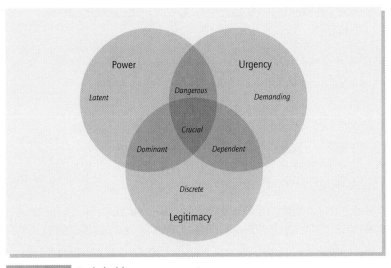

Figure 12.1 **Stakeholder management**   Source: after Mitchell, Agle and Wood (1997)

When to use it

With stakeholder management, a company can get a good idea of:

■ the most important (dominant) stakeholders for the company;

■ how the stakeholders relate to each other;

- what the various stakeholders contribute in their relationship with the company;
- what influencing power the stakeholders (should) have on the company;
- how the company could (and/or should) act in the stakeholders' interest.

How to use it

Stakeholder management begins with an inventory of the organisation's stakeholders. The different stakeholders are then grouped, e.g. into 'the environmental movement', 'the staff' or 'the government'. Not all stakeholders are equally important to an organisation. Based on a classification, the organisation can prioritise relations with certain stakeholders. The classification is based on three characteristics of the relationship:

- the power of the parties to influence the organisation;
- the legitimacy of the relationship and actions of the stakeholders with the organisation in terms of desirability, accuracy or appropriateness;
- the urgency of the demands on the organisation made by the interested party, and the extent to which the sensitivity requirement is crucial for that person.

Stakeholders that only score high on one of the three characteristics are called *latent stakeholders* (see also Figure 12.1). Stakeholders that score high on all three are crucial partners for the organisation. Their interests and concerns should always be considered by the organisation. To complete the assessment of the power of stakeholders, you should also look into the relative position of the stakeholder amongst all stakeholders. This can be done by mapping out (Figure 12.2):

	Relation	Coalition	Interest	Power	Priority
Employees					
Customers					
Suppliers					
Competitors					
Regulars					
Trade unions					
Labour unions					
...					

Figure 12.2 Stakeholder analysis

- the current relationship of the stakeholder with the organisation;

- the possible coalitions of the stakeholder with any of the other stakeholders;

- the position of the stakeholder in the environment/market in which the organisation is active;

- the power of the stakeholder;

- the priorities of the stakeholder.

After the inventory and any prioritisation, the interest of each stakeholder or interested group should be determined, as well as the concerns they might have about the organisation's new strategy. Based on these concerns, an estimate can be made regarding which stakeholders will support the organisation's objectives and which still have doubts. The supporters are called *movers*. They will probably contribute actively and will seek others to do so as well. Opponents are called *blockers*, and those who are not in favour but who do not oppose are called *floaters*. Depending on the importance given to the relationship with an interested party, targeted action should be chosen as soon as that person's attitude seems to be moving in the same direction as the organisation. *Movers* should be informed about the organisation's objectives and (planned) activities, so that they can contribute. *Floaters* can usually be won over by the organisation. With regard to their doubts, the organisation can explain to them how their interests will be served by its plans. The *blockers* will have to be consulted too. Find out what they perceive to be a threat and what the organisation can do to remove that perception. Often, too much attention is given to blockers and too little to floaters.

For all actions and communication with the different stakeholder groups, key performance indicators (KPIs) are chosen to monitor whether the action actually contributes to the mobilisation or the creation of a win–win situation with that stakeholder. A stakeholder action card is a suitable tool to keep track of these (see Figure 12.3). It is a practical tool that gives a good overview

Stakeholder (name)	Classification (latent-crucial)	Interest	Issue(s)	Coalition with	Attitude ('mover', 'floater', 'blocker')	Resistance/ response	Approach	KPI for approach	Monitoring method	Communication means

Figure 12.3 Stakeholder action card

of the interests, positions and roles of stakeholders, and the approach followed towards the stakeholder, as well as keeping track of progress and developments. It also allows further fine-tuning of actions and communication with the stakeholder when necessary.

The final analysis

Stakeholder management is an evergreen model that should always be used by any organisation. It can be particularly useful in any situation where there is resistance to (proposed) decisions, where there are changes among stakeholders and/or where a change in the actions, behaviour or attitude of one or more stakeholders of the organisation is required or would be beneficial. Stakeholder management provides practical guidance on how to convince any (internal or external) opponents and thus create support.

It is astonishing, however, how often in business a structured approach to the organisation's stakeholders is passed over. In a dynamic environment, a stakeholder analysis should be performed more frequently. Relevant groups change relatively rapidly, as do their power relations, interests and priorities. Not taking your stakeholders into consideration places the company's image and reputation in the public's mind at considerable risk and, with the advent of social media, this can bring your business to an immediate standstill.

References

Freeman, R.E. and Harrison, J.S. (2010) *Stakeholder Theory: The State of the Art.* Cambridge: Cambridge University Press.

Freeman, R.E. (2010) *Strategic Management: A Stakeholder Approach.* Cambridge: Cambridge University Press.

Mitchell, R. K., Agle, B.R. and Wood, D. J. (1997) 'Toward a theory of stakeholder identification and salience: Defining the principle of who and what really counts'. *Academy of Management Review* 22(4), 853–886.

part
five

Operations

13

Kaizen/Gemba

- **Why use it?** Kaizen is a tactical tool to help organisations strive for continuous improvement.

- **What does it do?** Kaizen eliminates waste and inefficiencies; it puts forward good housekeeping and use of standards.

- **When to use it?** Kaizen can be used to solve several types of problems: process inefficiencies, quality problems, large inventories, and delivery and lead-time problems.

- **What question will it help you answer?** How can I get my organisation to improve its performance and processes continuously?

The big picture

Kaizen literally means change (*kai*) to become good (*zen*). Key elements of kaizen are quality, effort, willingness to change and communication. The Gemba house, as the basis of kaizen, has five fundamental elements:

- teamwork
- personal discipline
- improved morale
- quality circles
- suggestions for improvement.

Based on this foundation, kaizen focuses on the elimination of *muda* (waste and inefficiencies (Figure 13.1).

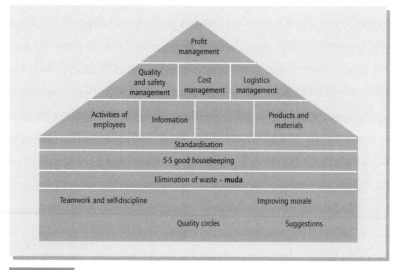

Figure 13.1 The Kaizen/Gemba model   Source: based on Imai (1997)

When to use it

Kaizen can be used to solve several types of problems: process inefficiencies, quality problems, large inventories, and delivery and lead-time problems. Employees are encouraged to come up with suggestions during weekly meetings (kaizen events) for small and large improvements. Kaizen suggests eliminating muda (waste and inefficiencies) first. The types of waste are:

- **Defective products.** Defects in quality prevent customers from accepting the manufactured product. The effort to create these defects is wasted. New waste management processes must be added in an effort to reclaim some value from an otherwise scrap product.

- **Over-production.** Over-production is the production or acquisition of items before they are actually required. It is the company's most dangerous waste, because it hides production problems. Over-production has to be stored, managed and protected.

- **Transportation.** Each time a product is moved, it runs the risk of being damaged, lost, delayed, etc., as well as being a cost with no added value. Transportation does contribute to the transformation of the product that the consumer is disposed to pay for.

- **Waiting.** Refers to the time spent by the workers waiting for resources to arrive, the queue for their products to empty, as well as the capital sunk into goods and services that have not yet been delivered to the customer. It is often the case that there are processes to manage this waiting.

- **Excess inventory.** Whether in the form of raw materials, work in progress (WIP) or finished goods, excess inventory represents a capital outlay that has not yet produced an income for either the producer or the consumer. If any of these three items are not being processed actively to add value, it is waste.

▥ **Motion.** In contrast to transportation, motion refers to the worker or equipment, and is represented by damage, wear and safety. It also includes the fixed assets and expenses incurred in the production process.

▥ **Extra processing.** Using a more expensive or otherwise valuable resource than is required for the task, or adding features that are included in the design but are not needed by the customer. There is a particular problem with this factor. People may need to perform tasks for which they are overqualified to maintain their competency. This training cost can be used to offset the waste associated with over-processing.

After the reduction of waste, good housekeeping is put forward, which comprises the 5-Ss:

1 *Seiri* – tidiness. Separate what is necessary for the work from what is not. This should help to simplify the work.

2 *Seiton* – orderliness. You can increase efficiency by making deliberate decisions regarding the allocation of materials, equipment, files, etc.

3 *Seiso* – cleanliness. Everyone should help to keep things clean, organised, and looking neat and attractive.

4 *Seiketsu* – standardised clean-up. The regularity and institutionalisation of keeping things clean and organised as part of 'visual management' is an effective means of continuous improvement.

5 *Shitsuke* – discipline. Personal responsibility for living up to the other 4-Ss can make or break the success of housekeeping.

The last building block of the Gemba house is standardisation. Standardisation of practices and institutionalisation of the 5-Ss will make it easier for everyone in the organisation to improve continuously, including newcomers. Top management plays an important role in guarding and acting for the widespread implementation and coordination of kaizen, the 5-S method, and the standardisation of work.

A correct implementation of the kaizen concept will lead to:

- Improved productivity
- Improved quality
- Better safety
- Faster delivery
- Lower costs
- Greater customer satisfaction
- Improved employee morale and job satisfaction.

How to use it

The following steps should be taken in kaizen events:

- Define the problem and the goal of the event.
- Analyse the facts.
- Generate possible solutions.
- Plan the solution.
- Implement the solution.
- Check and secure the solution.

It is important that the solution is checked and secured. In the final phase of a kaizen event, people start to seek opportunities for new kaizen events, which may hamper the process of embedding each improvement into operational practice.

The final analysis

The kaizen philosophy resonates well with the speed of change at operational levels in the organisation. The sustainability of the improvements proposed and implemented by people on the work floor is perhaps the strongest argument in favour of kaizen. Its sheer simplicity makes implementation easy, although some cultures may not be as receptive to the high level of self-discipline that the Japanese are able to maintain.

Kaizen has more potential in incremental change situations than in abrupt turnarounds. A culture focused on short-term success and big 'hits' is not the right environment for kaizen. Cooperation and widespread discipline at all levels of the organisation are the absolute keys to its success.

Reference

Imai, M. (1997) *Gemba Kaizen: A Commonsense, Low-cost Approach to Management.* London: McGraw-Hill.

Root cause analysis/ Pareto analysis

- **Why use it?** Root cause analysis (RCA) is a class of problem-solving methods aimed at identifying the root causes of problems or events. RCA is used to explain the variation in any process (or outcome of a process). A certain amount of variability is normal and does not necessarily cause significant disturbance. However, unwanted variation can cause serious losses or damage, delays and reduced productivity, especially if it occurs in critical processes.

- **What does it do?** Root cause analysis shows the causes of variations in a particular process. It helps to identify and cluster the causes of a certain problem or event and can help to further optimise the process.

- **When to use it?** The analysis is generally used in both financial analysis and in analysis of operations, such as business process reengineering (BPR) projects.

■ **What questions will it help you answer?** What is the problem? Which variation causes the most critical disturbance in the system under study? What are the issues that contributed to the problem (and their root causes) and which recommendations for solutions can be developed?

The big picture

Root cause analysis (RCA) is a class of problem-solving methods aimed at identifying the root causes of problems or events. It is based on the Ishikawa diagram (also fishbone diagram, or cause and effect diagram) named after its founder Kaoru Ishikawa (Figure 14.1a). The Ishikawa diagram shows the causes of a certain event. It was first used in the 1960s and is considered one of the seven basic tools of quality management, along with the histogram, Pareto chart, check sheet, control chart, flowchart and scatter diagram (Figure 14.1b). This principle is used in a root cause analysis and tries to explain the variations in a particular process. The analysis is generally used in both financial analysis and the analysis of operations.

When to use it

The RCA is used to explain the variation in any process (or outcome of a process). A certain amount of variability is normal and does not necessarily cause significant disturbance. However, unwanted variation can cause serious losses or damage, delays and reduced productivity, especially if it occurs in critical processes. The first essential step is to find the causes of variation and to quantify the effect. The main causes, which are generally easy to solve, should be taken care of first. The technique is particularly valuable for the analysis of critical processes that show undesirable variance.

How to use it

Root cause analysis usually starts with the formation of a project team, including managers, suppliers, customers and employees. Next, the team defines the problem and decides which variation causes the most critical disturbance in the system under study. Then the team maps out the process and identifies the issues

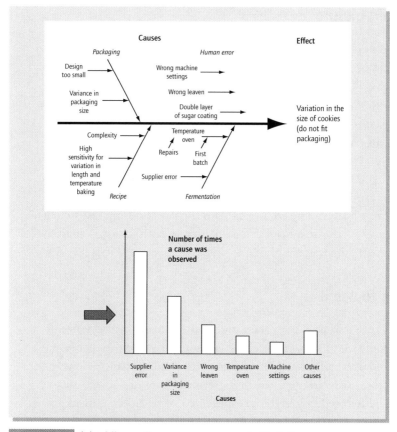

Figure 14.1 (a) Ishikawa diagram, or cause and effect diagram;
(b) Pareto diagram

that can cause variance in the data/evidence-gathering phase. Following this, issues that contributed to the problem are identified and their root causes found. However, the root causes might not be immediately evident, in which case brainstorming techniques are required. Subsequently, the root causes identified (usually large in number) are illustrated on a whiteboard in order to discuss and sharpen the findings. Recommendations for solutions now have to be developed and actually implemented.

The root causes can be organised by categorising them and by distinguishing between main root causes and smaller effects. This provides the input needed to draw a 'cause and effect' diagram. The diagram provides an overview of the possible causes of variation. It is essential to study the possible root cause in the diagram in detail, to see the extent of the cause of variation. The Pareto diagram is often used to present the findings. Analysing root causes generally shows that 80 per cent of the variation is caused by 20 per cent of the causes.

The final analysis

Root cause analysis is not a single, sharply defined methodology; there are many different tools, processes and philosophies regarding RCA. To maximise the effect of the use of RCA, it is advisable to start with the most critical processes and/or the most disturbing variances. This ensures that success will propagate the broader use of the model. However, try to avoid finding causes of variation that have only a small effect on the lead time, productivity or costs.

Reference

Blanchard, K.H., Schewe, C., Nelson, R. and Hiam, A. (1996) *Exploring the World of Business*. New York: WH Freeman.

Six sigma

- **Why use it?** Six sigma is used to improve the operational performance of an organisation by identifying and dealing with its deficiencies.

- **What does it do?** Six sigma claims that focusing on reduction of variation (beyond the sixth sigma) will solve process and business problems.

- **When to use it?** Six sigma projects can help achieve better financial results by improving quality and process reliability.

- **What questions will it help you answer?** Which financial improvements and cost savings can be achieved? What efficiencies can be gained by reducing variation in processes?

The big picture

The name six sigma originates from statistical terminology. Sigma is the mathematical symbol for standard deviation. Six sigma is a measure of the maximum number of defects that are allowed in a system. At the six sigma level, 99.999998 per cent of all products must be good, i.e. they fall within the tolerance limits (see Figure 15.1). This implies that no more than 3.4 defects are produced in one million opportunities. This level can be achieved by reducing the variation of the process and controlling it. To reach this quality level, the processes must be improved. However, process and quality improvements are not the ultimate goal – financial improvement is the goal.

Six sigma first became rooted at Motorola. To confront heavy Japanese competition, in 1987 Motorola started to focus on quality improvement. The engineers at Motorola decided that the norm they were using, of defects per 1000 units, was no longer appropriate. They therefore decided to measure the defects per million. Allied Signal and General Electric have perfected the

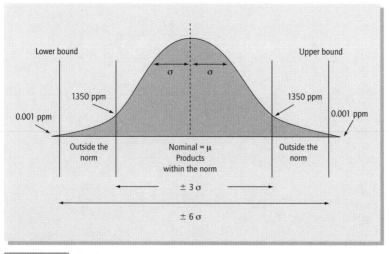

Figure 15.1 **Six sigma**   Source: after Van Assen, Notermans and Wigman (2007)

method. These firms have realised huge benefits by saving billions of dollars whilst improving customer satisfaction. Nowadays, six sigma projects are implemented not only in manufacturing firms, but also in the service industry.

Six sigma claims that focusing on reduction of variation will solve process and business problems. By using a set of statistical tools to understand the fluctuation of a process, management can begin to predict the expected outcome of that process. If the outcome is not satisfactory, other statistical tools can be used to further understand the elements that influence the process.

When to use it

Six sigma is used to improve the operational performance of an organisation by identifying and dealing with its deficiencies. Six sigma projects help to achieve better financial results by improving quality and process reliability. Every six sigma project has to focus on financial improvements and cost savings. The six sigma philosophy suggests that top management should not authorise a project that does not have a savings target of at least $175,000.

Six sigma is a top-down method where management has to communicate the goal of each project and audit it. The organisation's employees carry out the projects in a very structured way. The employees have one of the following roles:

- *Executive management champions* – the CEO or other key management team members that have a clear overview of the six sigma projects.
- *Master black belts* – external consultants who train the black belts and support six sigma projects.
- *Black belts* – the project leaders, who execute overall project management.
- *Green belts* – the project leaders of a part of a project, who implement six sigma projects.

▨ *Project teams* – each green belt has a project team. These employees are trained in the six sigma techniques.

The infrastructure of a six sigma project is unique for every organisation. Nevertheless, general requirements for successful implementation can be determined:

▨ A good understanding of statistical tools and techniques.

▨ Spending adequate resources on the definition phase.

▨ Spending adequate resources on the implementation phase.

▨ Effective management leadership and commitment.

▨ Undergoing a cultural change before implementation.

▨ Having an effective communication plan.

▨ Providing adequate training for the improvement teams.

▨ Having black belts with the ability to facilitate.

How to use it

Six sigma includes five steps: define, measure, analyse, improve and control (commonly known as DMAIC):

1 **Define.** First of all, a selection of the processes that must be improved has to take place, and the goals for improvement should be defined (SMART – specific, measurable, acceptable, realistic and time-specific).

2 **Measure.** After the definition phase, data are collected to evaluate the performance of the current process for future comparison.

3 **Analyse.** The difference between the current state and the desired state is determined in this phase.

4 **Improve.** Subsequently the process is optimised based on the analysis.

5 **Control.** The new improved processes should be controlled and formalised.

The final analysis

Six sigma comprises hard and soft techniques. The harder ones include a structured problem-solving approach, statistical process control tools (applied using DMAIC methodology) and project management techniques. The softer ones include people management, creativity and improvement motivation.

Benchmarking (see Chapter 6) is used in six sigma projects. The important characteristics of the product, the client, the internal process and the manufacturing system are compared with the products and processes of competitors. This is useful for financially orientated management, because the comparison at process level makes it possible to use six sigma techniques.

In six sigma projects, it is important to have vision and enthusiasm, but a requirement for successful projects is a well-defined infrastructure for training, support and project coordination.

References

Breyfogle III, F.W. (2003) *Implementing Six Sigma: Smarter Solutions using Statistical Methods*. Hoboken, New Jersey: John Wiley & Sons.

Van Assen, M.F., Notermans, R. and Wigman, J. (2007) *Operational Excellence New Style*. The Hague: Academic Service [in Dutch: *Operational Excellence nieuwe stijl*].

part

six

Innovation

16

Disruptive innovation

- **Why use it?** Using disruptive innovation helps firms work out what they can do to avoid displacement brought on by radical, technological innovations or how they can pursue such innovations themselves.

- **What does it do?** Disruptive innovation is a method that helps identify and manage potentially disruptive innovations. Although the concept of disruptive innovation was received as almost being a radical innovation in itself, it is a concept that can help explain certain developments in markets and industries.

- **When to use it?** Disruptive innovation is most useful in highly dynamic markets and in situations where new technologies or technological innovations are emerging.

- **What question will it help you answer?** What are possible disruptive innovations that will change the market and lead to new products or services (potentially) designed for new sets of customers?

The big picture

Introduced by Joseph Bowyer and Clayton Christenson in their 1995 article, a disruptive innovation is an innovation that leads to a product or service designed for a new set of customers. By contrast, sustaining innovations are typically innovations in a new technology or application, whereas disruptive innovations change entire markets (Figure 16.1).

When to use it

The use of disruptive innovation helps to answer the question: what can firms do to avoid displacement brought on by radical, technological innovations? Contrary to the popular belief that established companies are unaware of (disruptive) innovations, most companies are hindered by their business environment (or value network) from pursuing them when they first arise. All too often, emerging, potentially disruptive innovations are – like most innovations – not profitable enough at first, and their development can take scarce resources away from other innovations

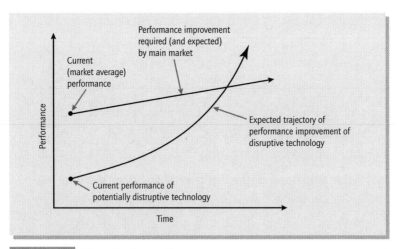

Figure 16.1 **Disruptive innovation**   Source: based on Bowyer and Christensen (1995)

(which are also needed to compete against the current competition). Start-up firms seem not to be hindered in this way and are often disruptive to established firms. Generally there are two types of disruptive innovation:

▪ **Low-end disruption** targets segments of the market that are not willing to pay a premium for extra performance. Often these are the least profitable customers. For a disruptive innovation, this is a good segment to start off with, as it is 'below the radar' of established firms and allows one to gain a (niche) position in a market. From this position, the disrupting party will seek to improve its profit margin and market position. This requires further innovation to be able to move upmarket and enter the segments where the customer is willing to pay more for greater performance. Once most segments are served, the disruptive party has driven most established companies out of the market and has set the new standard with the once disruptive technology. In some markets, e.g. data storage or computing hardware, developments and innovations speedily follow one another, showing a pattern of this type of disruption.

▪ **New market disruption** targets customers who have needs that were previously unserved by existing incumbents, for instance a new or emerging market segment.

How to use it

Disruptive innovation is a method that helps identify and manage potentially disruptive innovations. This is different from just research and development (R&D) management or technology development. The difference is mainly in the scope. Where few technologies are intrinsically disruptive or sustaining in character, a disruptive innovation is identified by the business model that the technology enables. In their article, Bowyer and Christensen suggest the following guidelines on how to foster disruptive innovations within any company:

- Determine whether the innovation is disruptive or sustaining.
- Define the strategic significance of the disruptive innovation.
- Locate the market for the disruptive innovation.
- Place responsibility for building business with the disruptive innovation in an independent organisation.
- Keep the disruptive innovation independent: do not integrate it into mainstream business activities as this tends to lower the disruptive power of the innovation.

The final analysis

Although the concept of disruptive innovation was first received almost as a radical innovation itself, it helps to explain developments in markets and industries. Similar to Moore's law (i.e. the observation of Gordon Moore, former CEO of Intel, that the number of transistors on integrated circuits doubles approximately every 2 years), disruptive innovation is best used descriptively, although it was presented as a method for spotting and cultivating disruptive technologies.

Disruptive innovation is built on a lot of assumptions, starting with the assumption that one can know which technology has the potential to be disruptive before it is readily available on the market and/or has a performance that is equal to that of the market average of currently available technologies. Next there is the assumption that the performance improvement that is required and expected by the market – based on currently available technologies – is known. The most important assumption is that the market will adopt a technology that outperforms not only the current market average but also the customers' expectations. It assumes that customers will be in awe and that the market will shift (or a new market will be created) in response to the performance of this technology.

With regard to this latter assumption, disruptive innovation does not take into account any aspects other than the technology's performance as being decisive for the adoption of the new technology by customers. Assessing the expected trajectory of performance improvement of the potential disruptive technology might better be done in conjunction with other management models, incorporating other market (entry) related factors.

References

Bowyer, J.L and Christensen, C.M. (1995) 'Disruptive technologies: Catching the wave'. *Harvard Business Review* 73(1), 43–53.

Christensen, C.M. (1997) *The Innovators Dilemma: When New Technologies Cause Great Firms to Fail.* Boston MA: Harvard Business School Press.

Leifer, R., McDermott, C.M., O'Connor, C.G., Peters, L.S., Rice, M.P. and Veryzer, R.W. (2000) *Radical Innovation: How Mature Companies Can Outsmart Upstarts.* Boston MA: Harvard Business School Press.

chapter

17

Innovation circle

- **Why use it?** The innovation circle is a model for analysing and managing the life cycle of a new innovation.

- **What does it do?** Innovation processes are often complex and not easy to manage. This model identifies which phases in the life cycle of an innovation are the most important and therefore in greatest need of management focus and attention.

- **When to use it?** The innovation circle can be used to manage the life cycles of a variety of innovations. As the innovation process is divided into successive phases, management attention can be more easily directed to areas of need during the life cycle of the innovation.

- **What question will it help you answer?** How can I oversee and manage the different stages of the innovation process and focus on creating not only new products, but also products that are commercially interesting?

The big picture

The innovation circle is a model for efficiently analysing and successively managing the life cycle of a new innovation. Innovation – that is, the creation of new products, processes and services – is an essential process for creating a (long-term) competitive advantage. However, innovation processes are often complex and not easy to manage. This model identifies which phases in the life cycle of an innovation are the most important and in greatest need of management focus and attention.

The creation of new products, processes and services is a key challenge for management. The innovation circle identifies three main phases that are necessary to manage the life cycle of an innovation successfully – *creation*, *implementation* and *capitalisation* (Figure 17.1):

1 **The creation phase.** The 'seeds' of new products, processes and services are discovered and organised in the creation phase. This phase comprises three steps:

  (i) **Receive incentives** – in this step, the external incentives that initiate the innovation process are distinguished and interpreted. Examples of external incentives are diminishing growth, weakening of the brand, the decline of customer satisfaction and the development of new technologies (or other areas of knowledge).

  (ii) **Generate ideas** – in this step, the generation of new ideas is the key. The external stimuli (the incentives received) provide the initiative to create new (product) ideas. Idea creation can be stimulated by a creative climate in which variety and exploration stand central, and where chaos and energy are the main drivers. For example, brainstorming sessions in which out-of-the-box thinking is stimulated can result in the creation of (many) new ideas. The best new ideas will be selected and go through to the next phase. During this process, the focus should be on the

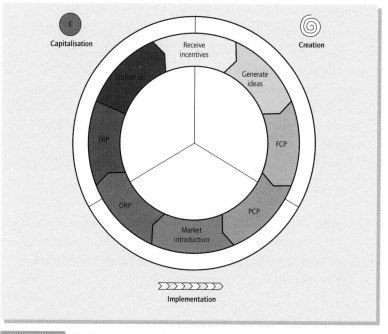

Source: after Krebbekx and De Wolf (2008)

Figure 17.1 **The innovation circle**

needs of customers. Creation of (new) value for customers is the ultimate goal. The customer value can be recognised by identifying the rewards (return on investment), risks (technological and market) and resources (investment).

(iii) **Function creation process (FCP)** – in this step, the ideas are transformed into manageable functions. In addition, the risks are identified and can therefore be controlled. If the functions are clear, it is time to move on to the next phase.

2 **The implementation phase.** In this phase, the new product, process or service is further developed. The market introduction is prepared and executed. This phase is divided into two steps:

(i) **Product creation process (PCP)** – during the PCP, the new product and/or service is developed from the specifications created during the FCP phase. In this step, the product is tested, e.g. by developing a prototype and running demos.

(ii) **Market introduction** – in this step, all aspects of the market introduction are managed. This also implies the preparation of the following phase (see ORP below).

3 **The capitalisation phase.** In this final phase, the commercialisation of the new product, process and/or service is managed. This phase addresses the issue of how to create value (money) for the firm from the innovation(s). It is divided into three steps, in which operational excellence is key:

(i) **Order realisation process (ORP)** – in this step, the management of the continuous, repeating stream of product deliveries is executed. This is concerned with the management of the logistics and production of the new product. Integration with the existing logistics and the production of current products is crucial to generate synergy and scale advantages.

(ii) **Service realisation process (SRP)** – in this step, the management of providing (additional) services is undertaken. New services have to be integrated into the current service process.

(iii) **Utilisation** – the final step of the innovation circle concerns the management of the new product's revenues. This implies the continued preservation of the product's margin. Reductions in production costs and small adjustments to the product are ways in which the margin of a product can be preserved. This phase ends when the life cycle of the product has ended.

When to use it

The innovation circle can be used to manage the life cycles of a variety of innovations without overlooking relevant aspects of the innovation process. As the innovation process is divided into successive phases, management attention can be more easily directed to the correct subject during the life cycle of the innovation.

How to use it

The three phases of the innovation circle – creation, implementation and capitalisation – should be managed differently. In the creation phase, the search for new ideas is dominant. In this phase, management is directed towards managing creativity, but not in the same way as programme and project management, as search processes are not directed at a clear goal (clear goals are prerequisites in programme and project management). Rather, this phase can be managed by starting parallel research to explore different solutions. This iterative process ends when, with a degree of certainty, the most appropriate solution to the problem is found.

The implementation phase can be managed more tightly. The goal of this phase is clear from the outset and includes the different functions of the product, process and/or service. The necessary resources (mainly time and money) are therefore reasonably well known and manageable. This phase can be managed well by project management.

In the capitalisation phase, the new product, process and/or service is integrated into the ongoing operation, for which operational excellence programmes are appropriate.

The final analysis

The innovation circle is an analytical tool for managing an innovation process that provides a structure for overseeing its inherent complexity. Various analytical tools for new product management have been developed during the past few decades. The best-known tool is probably the Stage-Gate model (see Chapter 18). The Stage-Gate model and the innovation circle are comparable, in that they both provide an approach to managing the different stages of an innovation process. However, the innovation circle differs from the Stage-Gate model in two ways.

First, the innovation circle directs more attention to the capitalisation phase. As such, management is not only focused on creating new products, but also on the creation of new products that are commercially interesting, and which can be integrated into the present operational infrastructure. Secondly, the innovation circle differs because of its shape. It represents a continuous process, implying that innovation should not stop at the end of a product's life cycle. The end of a product can be a powerful incentive for new product ideas.

References

Camps, T.W., de Wolf, W. and van den Berg, G. (2011) *Success!! Ten Lessons in Innovation.* Utrecht: Berenschot [in Dutch: *Geslaagd! 10 Lessen in Innovatie*].

Krebbekx, J. and de Wolf, W. (2008) *Innovation in Dutch Industry: Towards Excellence in Product Development.* Utrecht: Berenschot [in Dutch: *Innovatie Nederlandse Industrie*].

18

Stage-Gate model

■ **Why use it?** The Stage-Gate model is based on the belief that product innovation begins with ideas and ends once a product is successfully launched into the market. The model provides quality control check points in the process, which contribute to three goals: ensuring quality of execution, evaluating business rationale and allocating resources.

■ **What does it do?** The Stage-Gate model, also referred to as the Phase-Gate model, takes the often complex and chaotic process of developing an idea (e.g. for a new technology, a new product or a process improvement) from inception to launch and divides it into stages or phases (where project activities are conducted), separated by gates (where business evaluations and 'go/ kill' decisions are made). At each gate, the continuation of the process is decided on.

- **When to use it?** Most organisations suffer from having far too many projects in their product and technology development pipelines for the limited resources available. A structured approach with clearly stated stages and gates at which a project can be stopped, help to prune the development portfolio of weak projects and deal with a gridlocked pipeline.

- **What question will it help you answer?** How can I ensure that the right projects are done correctly?

The big picture

The Stage-Gate model, also referred to as the Phase-Gate model, takes the often complex and chaotic process of developing an idea (e.g. for a new technology, a new product or a process improvement) from inception to launch and divides it into stages or phases (where project activities are conducted), separated by gates (where business evaluations and 'go/kill' decisions are made). At each gate, the continuation of the process is decided on. Originating in the chemical industry, the use of funnel tools in decision-making when dealing with new technology and product development was further developed by institutions like NASA. In the mid-1990s, Robert Cooper and Scott Edgett, two Canadian scholars, developed the Stage-Gate model as it is known today (Figure 18.1).

When to use it

The Stage-Gate model is based on the belief that product innovation begins with ideas and ends once a product is successfully launched into the market. In its entirety, Stage-Gate incorporates pre-development activities (business justification and preliminary feasibilities), development activities (technical, marketing and operations development) and commercialisation activities (market launch and post-launch learning) into one complete, robust process. Most firms suffer from having far too many projects in their product and technology development pipelines for the limited resources available. A structured approach with clearly stated stages and gates at which a project can be stopped helps to prune the development portfolio of weak projects and deal with a gridlocked pipeline. In particular, the gates serve as quality control checkpoints in the process. They contribute to three goals: ensuring quality of execution, evaluating business rationale and allocating resources. In this way, the Stage-Gate model tries to ensure the right projects are done correctly.

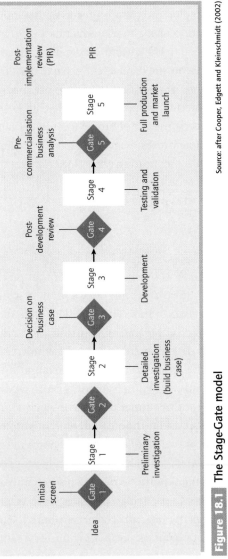

Figure 18.1 The Stage-Gate model

Source: after Cooper, Edgett and Kleinschmidt (2002)

How to use it

A generic Stage-Gate model has five phases and five gates. Ahead of the first phase is a preliminary or ideation phase called discovery. The result of this phase is an idea for a new technology or new product to be developed. This idea is then presented at the first gate: the initial screen. When it meets the requirements set at this gate, such as relevance to the company's aspired market position and/or complementarity within the product portfolio, the idea is taken on and a project is formulated. This project then – generically – moves through five phases:

- **Scoping** – stating the project definition, project justification and the proposed plan for development. Also, stating the initial thoughts on application(s) of, target customers for and benefits from the idea.

- **Build business case** – once past the second gate, the business rationale of the project is to be proven. By investigating the potential market(s) and potential application(s), the potential benefits offered by the idea (e.g. for a new technology or product) to potential customers are outlined. The comparative advantage over the competition and substitutes should also be stated. The feasibility of the new product and technology is also to be proven.

- **Development** – after passing the third gate, where management has reviewed the business rationale of the project, the actual detailed design and development of the new product or new technology take place. This often includes the design of the operations or production process required for eventual full-scale production.

- **Testing and validation** – after passing the fourth gate, where the technical feasibility (proof-of-concept and/or prototypes) is reviewed, tests or trials in the marketplace, laboratory and plant take place to verify and validate the proposed new product or technology and its associated brand/marketing plan and production/operations plan.

- **Launch** – once past the fifth gate, where the commercial feasibility (of the validated product) is reviewed, the new product or technology is commercialised and operations or production, marketing and selling start at full scale.

Often after the fifth phase there is an evaluation of the development process and of the launch. This evaluation is also known as the post-launch or post-implementation review.

The final analysis

The Stage-Gate model has a number of advantages that typically result from its ability to identify problems and assess progress before the project's conclusion. Poor projects can be quickly rejected by disciplined use of the model.

The Stage-Gate model can easily be used in conjunction with financial (project) valuation methods such as net present value (see Chapter 9) and technology assessment methods such as technology readiness levels to base decision-making on quantitative analysis of the feasibility and attractiveness of developing potential product ideas. Another advantage of the model is that, at each gate, there is an opportunity to interact with the project's executive sponsors and other stakeholders with regard to the progress and importance of a project.

An inherent disadvantage of the Stage-Gate model is that it structures the process of new product or technology development, which might interfere with creativity and innovation. The model regards these processes as linear, although in reality many creative and research-driven projects are largely iterative processes.

References

Cooper, R.G., Edgett, S.J. and Kleinschmidt, E.J. (2002) *Portfolio Management for New Products*. Reading: Perseus Books.

Cooper, R.G. (2011) *Winning at New Products: Creating Value through Innovation*, 3rd edn. Philadelphia PA: Basic Books.

European Industrial Research Management Association (EIRMA) (2002) No. 59: *Project Portfolio* Management. Paris: EIRMA.

Stage-Gate International: **www.stage-gate.com**

part

seven

Change management

Eight phases of change (Kotter)

- **Why use it?** Kotters's eight phases of change is a systematic approach to achieving successful, sustainable change by breaking down the change process into eight phases.

- **What does it do?** The eight phases of change approach provides a systematic tool for leading the change process, enabling people to bring about lasting changes within their organisations, and avoiding (possibly) fatal mistakes.

- **When to use it?** This approach can be used when implementing changes in the organisation that need to last and that require an efficient implementation process.

- **What question will it help you answer?** How can I avoid making common mistakes during change processes (for example allowing complacency, underestimating the need for a clear vision and failing to create short-term wins) by understanding why organisations change, and the numerous steps required to realise the change?

The big picture

Kotters's eight phases of change is a systematic approach to achieving successful, sustainable change by breaking down the change process into eight phases (see Figure 19.1). It is based on a study of more than 100 companies that have been through a change process. Kotter (1990, 1995) found that the most common mistakes made during change processes are allowing: too much complacency; failing to create a substantial coalition; under-estimating the need for a clear vision; failing to communicate the vision clearly; permitting road blocks; failing to create short-term wins; declaring victory too soon; and not anchoring changes in the corporate culture. Kotter claims that these errors can be avoided by understanding why organisations change, and the numerous steps required to realise the change.

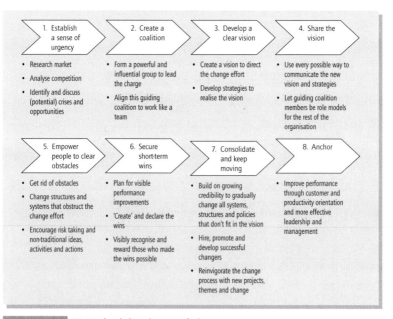

Figure 19.1 Kotter's eight phases of change

When to use it

In today's dynamic business world, the ability to lead change has become an important requirement for creating and maintaining success in all organisations. Kotter makes a clear distinction between leading change and managing it. He states that management consists of a set of processes that keep a complex system of people and technology running smoothly. Leadership, on the other hand, defines the future, aligns people with that vision and inspires them to pursue it. The eight phases of change approach provides a systematic tool for leading that process, enabling people to bring about lasting changes within their organisations, and avoiding (possibly) fatal mistakes.

How to use it

Kotter stresses the importance of going through all eight phases as described in detail in the following list. However, if running multiple change projects, it is likely that an organisation will find itself in more than one phase of the model at any given time. The phases are as follows:

1 **Establish a sense of urgency.** In dealing with complacency, it is important to eliminate false signs of security. Management has to ensure that the relevant people feel a sense of urgency due to a crisis or a potential crisis, and that they are convinced that doing business as usual is no longer an acceptable option.

2 **Create a coalition.** A strong guiding coalition is needed in order to create change in an organisation. The members of this group need to recognise the value of the envisaged change, and must share trust and commitment. Furthermore, they should possess the credibility, skills, connections, reputations, and formal authority to provide change leadership.

3 **Develop a clear vision.** Vision is a central component in leading change. It is the bridge between current and future states, providing a sense of direction and aligning efforts. The best visions are sensible, clear, simple, elevating and situation-specific.

4 **Share the vision.** Communicating the vision to everyone involved is crucial if everyone is to understand and commit to the change. Communicating the vision inadequately and with inconsistent messages are both major pitfalls that hinder successful change.

5 **Empower people to clear obstacles.** The guiding coalition should remove any barriers to action that may be entrenched in the organisational processes and structures, or exist in the perception of employees. This allows everyone to participate in the change effort.

6 **Generate short-term wins.** Change may take time and significant effort. Therefore, people should be encouraged and endorsed by creating short-term wins. These wins should be unambiguous, visible to many, and closely related to the change effort.

7 **Consolidate and keep moving.** Build momentum by consolidating the accomplished gains, using them as stepping stones to greater wins and enabling people to generate new activities related to the vision driving the effort.

8 **Anchor new approaches in culture.** Having made effective changes, leaders must now make the changes permanent and prevent things from going back to the way they were. Kotter states that the real key to lasting change is in changing the corporate culture itself, through consistency of successful action over a sufficient period.

The final analysis

Kotter does not shy away from the complexity of organisational change by offering a simplistic approach. He recognises that there are many ways of making mistakes in change efforts. In fact, even successful change efforts are messy and full of surprises. However, anyone attempting to make a change effort in an organisational setting should consider Kotter's model precisely in order to prevent making the 'common mistakes' and be able to face challenges specific to the particular change effort in hand.

References

Kotter, J.P. (1990) *A Force for Change: How Leadership Differs from Management*. New York: Free Press.

Kotter, J.P. (1996) *Leading Change*. Cambridge MA: Harvard Business School Press.

Kotter, J.P. (2002) *The Heart of Change: Real-life Stories of How People Change their Organisations*. Cambridge MA: Harvard Business School Press.

20

Team roles (Belbin)

- **Why use it?** Effective teams consist of members with different roles. For any task, a combination of roles will form the most effective team.

- **What does it do?** With a profile of each team member's ability to fulfil one or more roles, it is possible to detect the potential under- or over-representation of certain roles in the team. If necessary, management may decide to use this information to pay greater attention to certain roles during the execution of team tasks, and to make arrangements regarding the way in which the team members work together.

- **When to use it?** Analysis of (the roles of) team members using the Belbin model is especially useful in situations where a team must be created that can undertake an assignment requiring a certain set of skills and combination of roles, or to optimise cooperation in an existing team.

- **What question will it help you answer?** How can I compose a more flexible, complementary and stronger team?

The big picture

Belbin (1985) distinguishes nine complementary roles of successful business teams that can be classified as follows:

People-orientated roles	Cerebral roles	Action-orientated roles
1. Coordinator	4. 'Plant'/creator/inventor	7. Shaper
2. Team worker	5. Monitor/evaluator	8. Implementer
3. Resource investigator	6. Specialist	9. Finisher

1 The **coordinator** is a mature and confident person. He or she probably brings experience as a chairperson or leader of some kind to the table. Coordinators clarify goals, encourage decision-making and delegate tasks, but can, however, be manipulative or bossy, especially when they let others do work that could and should be done by themselves.

2 The **team worker** is cooperative, mild, perceptive and diplomatic – in a nutshell, everybody's friend. Team workers listen, build, balance and avert friction. Their inherent indecisiveness surfaces in crunch situations. The doers in the team tend to think team workers talk too much.

3 The **resource investigator** is an enthusiastic, communicative extrovert who explores opportunities and develops contacts that he or she thinks will benefit him/her now or later. Although opportunistic and optimistic, resource investigators tend to have a short span of attention and they quickly lose interest.

4 The **'plant'** is Belbin's name for the creator or inventor. Plants are creative and imaginative, even brilliant at times. Their unorthodox thinking helps to solve difficult problems. Plants ignore incidentals and are too preoccupied to communicate effectively. The problem is that this self-aware genius has a tendency to get other team members' backs up.

5 The **monitor** evaluates actions and ponders the strategy. Monitors are sober yet discerning, and keep track of progress. They oversee all options and judge accurately, but lack drive and the ability to inspire others.

6 The **specialist** is a single-minded, dedicated self-starter. Specialists provide rare knowledge and skills, and therefore their contribution is limited to a narrow front. These people get a kick out of technicalities and need to be told to get to the point.

7 The **shaper** is challenging, dynamic and thrives on pressure. Shapers have the drive and courage to overcome obstacles, see no evil and hear no evil. They might rub people up the wrong way in their zealous efforts get things going.

8 The **implementer** is a disciplined, reliable, conservative and efficient person who turns ideas into practical actions. Once at work, implementer will keep going and stick to the plan. They person might be a little rigid and unwilling to adopt alternative approaches or solutions along the way.

9 The **finisher** is meticulous, punctual, conscientious and anxious to make sure that everything turns out perfectly. Finishers deliver on time, but sometimes worry too much. They certainly hate to delegate work. Nobody else seems to understand that it has to be perfect.

When to use it

Analysis of (the roles of) team members using the Belbin model is especially useful in situations where a team must be created that can undertake an assignment requiring a certain set of skills and combination of roles, or in order to optimise cooperation in an existing team.

To make use of the model, members of a prospective team should first determine which roles they can and want to fulfil. Each member should subsequently be assessed to see whether, and to what extent, he or she could play one or more of the nine roles.

Such an assessment is in itself beneficial, in that it encourages individuals to take a closer look at their own strengths and weaknesses, at those of the other team members, and at their cooperation. These can then be exploited or corrected as necessary, resulting ultimately in a more flexible, complementary and stronger team.

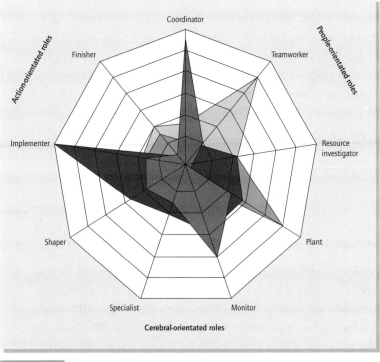

Figure 20.1 Belbin's complementary roles plotted

Source: based on Belbin (1985)

How to use it

The assessment can be done in various ways:

- self-assessment (apply scores, rank, rate or distribute weights), possibly supervised by a third party;
- team assessment (let the team work on a small assignment or game, and let the members grade each other);
- assessment by an unprejudiced individual such as a mentor, a former team member, or perhaps a co-worker or supervisor.

With a profile of each team member's ability to fulfil one or more roles, it is possible to detect the potential under- or over-representation of certain roles in the team (see Figure 20.1). If necessary, management may decide to use this information to pay greater attention to certain roles during the execution of team tasks and to make arrangements regarding the way in which the team members work together.

The final analysis

The way Belbin observes teams and the roles of team members assumes that there is an objective basis for assessing team members, but this is open to debate. A team assessment based on Belbin's team roles is nonetheless a very useful exercise. People will recognise themselves and team dynamics in this model.

Whilst the different roles are complementary, it can be fatal to have too many representatives of the same type of role in one team: too many coordinators in the same team results in a clash, and having two monitors in the same team may hold up a team's progress because they keep waiting for others to take action.

The model does not address the importance of interpersonal relationships within a team. Many teams that look good on paper fail to function properly in practice because they do not 'click'. The reverse is also true: for example, a person who has no history of being a coordinator may rise to the occasion and fill a vacuum.

Reference

Belbin, R.M. (1985) *Management Teams: Why they Succeed or Fail.* London: Heinemann.

21

The Deming cycle: plan–do–check–act

- **Why use it?** The Deming cycle, or plan-do-check-act (PDCA) cycle is a method to structure and effectively manage improvement and change projects.

- **What does it do?** PDCA leads you through a logical sequence of four repetitive steps for continuous improvement and learning: planning ('plan') the improvement of an activity should be followed by execution of the activity ('do') according to the plan. One should then measure and study ('check') the results and the improvement. Action should then be taken ('act') towards adapting the objectives and/or improvement. The consequent learning should be implemented in planning the new activities.

- **When to use it?** The PDCA cycle allows an organisation to manage improvement initiatives in a disciplined way.

■ **What question will it help you answer?** How can I specify my objectives, activities and desired results and manage the improvements systematically and consistently?

The big picture

The Deming (or plan–do–check–act, PDCA) cycle is a method to structure improvement and change projects. It refers to a logical sequence of four repetitive steps for continuous improvement and learning: *plan*, *do*, *check* and *act*. Planning ('plan') the improvement of an activity should be followed by execution of the activity ('do') according to the plan. One should then measure and study ('check') the results and the improvement. Action should then be taken ('act') towards adapting the objectives and/ or improvement. The consequent learning should be implemented in planning the new activities (Figure 21.1).

When to use it

The PDCA cycle allows an organisation to manage improvement initiatives in a disciplined way. When confronted with this model for the first time, many will realise that they are steering, but not

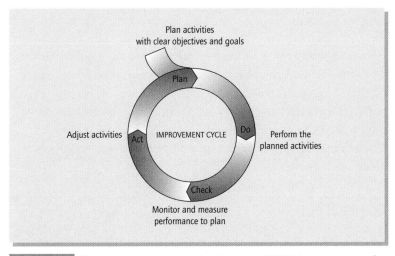

Figure 21.1   The Deming cycle: plan-do-check-act (PDCA). Four stages of a single cycle

Source: based on Walton and Deming (1986)

really managing their organisation. It can be used to structure and discipline the process of continuous improvement. Pictorially, the process of improvement may look as if one were rolling the PDCA wheel uphill. Each problem-solving cycle corresponds to a PDCA cycle (Figure 21.2).

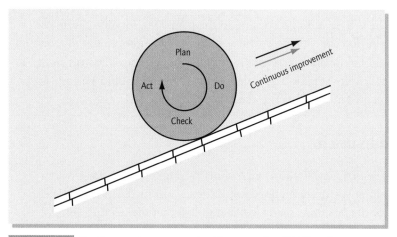

Figure 21.2 Continuous improvement with successive PDCA cycles

It is important to teach all the managers who have to work with this improvement method how to use the cycle. By making explicit use of the PDCA cycle, people will become aware of the improvements and benefits. This will encourage people to continue with the improvement projects. The cycle can be applied to different subjects, e.g. to achieving a mission, objectives, control points or in training.

How to use it

Go through the four steps systematically when pursuing improvement in specified activities.

1. Plan

Plan ahead for change. Analyse the current situation and the potential impact of any adjustments before you do anything else. Predict the various results expected, with or without the theory. How can you measure the impact when the desired result has been achieved? Plan to include result measurement in the execution. Make an implementation plan with assigned responsibilities for participants.

Experience shows that it is useful to ask the following questions:

- What are we trying to achieve?
- How can this be linked to the higher purpose of our organisation?
- Who is going to be affected?
- Where will it happen?
- When will it happen?
- What is the step-by-step procedure?
- How can we measure the improvement, if at all?

2. Do

When executing the plan, you must take small steps in controlled circumstances in order to be able to attribute improvements (or failures) to the planned changes in the activity.

3. Check

Check the results of your experiment. Was the desired result achieved? Analyse why success is realised – and if not, find out why not.

4. Act

Take action when results are not as desired. Try to standardise procedures by including those actions that have already been proved to contribute to success and eliminating those that do not contribute. Or, in the event that the result proved to be other than what was desired, use the experience as input for new attempts at improvement.

The final analysis

Many organisations are unable to specify objectives, activities and desired results, let alone manage their own improvements systematically and consistently, with or without the PDCA cycle. In addition, it requires discipline to practise the whole PDCA cycle, to stop firefighting and to stop undertaking only plan–do–plan–do. There have been several adaptations of the PDCA cycle. For example, plan can be split into 'determine goals and targets' and 'determine methods of reaching goals'; and 'do' can be split into 'training and education' and 'implementation'. The PDCA cycle constitutes an important part of the kaizen thinking described in this book (see Chapter 13).

Reference

Walton, M. and Deming, W.E. (1986) *The Deming Management Method.* New York: Dodd.

part

eight

Leadership and management

Competing values

- **Why use it?** The competing values framework is a model for judging the effectiveness of organisations, but it can also be used to assess and define supervision and management development programmes.

- **What does it do?** Using the model you will gain a better understanding of organisational effectiveness criteria. Based on three organisational dilemmas, your organisation is plotted against one of four basic models of (organisational and managerial) effectiveness.

- **When to use it?** In an organisational context, the framework can be used in four ways: to develop supervision and management development programmes, to understand various organisational functions and processes, to examine organisational gaps and to diagnose an organisation's culture.

- **What question will it help you answer?** How can I increase my organisational and managerial effectiveness? What are the unseen values for which people and organisations live and die?

The big picture

The competing values framework is a model for judging the effectiveness of organisations (Quinn and Rohrbaugh, 1983), but it can also be used to assess and define supervision and management development programmes. The study by Quinn and Rohrbaugh (1983) was an attempt to gain a better understanding of organisational effectiveness criteria, which resulted in a multi-dimensional scaling or spatial model with three dimensions (Figure 22.1):

■ internal vs external focus of the organisation;

■ flexibility vs stability of the organisation;

■ process vs goals orientation (the means to achieving the end).

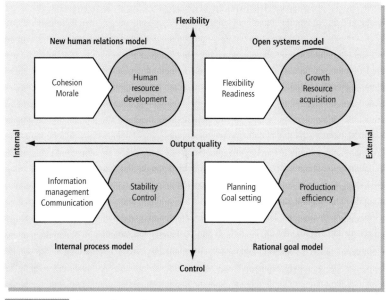

Figure 22.1 Competing values   Source: based on Quinn and Rohrbaugh (1983)

When to use it

In an organisational context, the framework can be used in four ways:

- to develop supervision and management development programmes;
- to understand various organisational functions and processes;
- to examine organisational gaps;
- to diagnose an organisation's culture.

How to use it

The dimensions of the model reflect well-known organisational dilemmas. The first dimension (internal vs external organisational focus) represents a basic organisational dilemma in which, at one end of the scale, the organisation is viewed as a socio-technical entity, and at the other as a logically designed tool for accomplishing business goals.

Flexibility vs stability is another basic organisational dilemma. Order and control do not mix well with innovation and change. Many social theorists have (successfully) argued for authority, structure and coordination, while others have found evidence for individual initiative and organisational adaptability.

Finally, a study of organisational effectiveness cannot be complete without observation of the tendency of means, methods, procedures and rules to become functionally autonomous, i.e. to become goals in themselves.

The integration of these dimensions results in four basic models of organisational effectiveness:

1 **Internal process model** – based on hierarchy, with an emphasis on measurement, documentation and information management. These processes bring stability and control. Hierarchies

seem to function best when the task at hand is well understood and when time is not an important factor.

2 **Open systems model** – based on an organic system, with an
emphasis on adaptability, readiness, growth, resource acquisition and external support. These processes bring innovation
and creativity. People are not controlled but inspired.

3 **Rational goal model** – based on profit, with an emphasis on
rational action. It assumes that planning and goal-setting
results in productivity and efficiency. Tasks are clarified, objectives are set, and action is taken.

4 **Human relations model** – based on cohesion and morale, with
an emphasis on human resources and training. People are seen
not as isolated individuals, but as cooperating members of a
common social system with a common stake in what happens.

While the models seem to be four entirely different perspectives
or domains, they can be viewed as closely related and interwoven.
They are four sub-domains of a larger construct: organisational
and managerial effectiveness. The four models in the framework
represent the unseen values for which people, programmes, policies and organisations live and die.

The final analysis

The debate surrounding the model that describes organisations and the issues they face is ongoing. In an effort to derive a
framework for organisational analysis, Quinn and Rohrbaugh
approached a large number of organisational researchers and
experts to determine the key dimensions of organisational
issues. The fact that the three dimensions of the model so closely
describe three major areas of debate and research indicates that
the authors have been quite successful in their effort to provide a
framework for organisational effectiveness.

In anticipation of criticism, Quinn and Rohrbaugh agree that the
spatial model is a type of oxymoron: a combination of seemingly

contradictory and simple concepts. However, the theoretical paradoxes are not necessarily empirical opposites. They argue that an organisation might be cohesive and productive, or stable as well as flexible. Does its apparent simplicity limit the scope of the model? Quinn and Rohrbaugh would seem to argue the contrary, as they state that the process of creating the model is, in itself, productive. Quinn and Rohrbaugh present a number of alternative methods for comparing and describing their model; for instance, using Parson's functional prerequisites model, in which core values, coordination mechanisms and organisational structures are presented.

References

O'Neill, R.M and Quinn, R.E. (1993) 'Editor's Note: Applications of the competing values framework'. *Human Resource Management* 32(1), 1–7.

Quinn, R.E. and Rohrbaugh, J. (1983) 'A spatial model of effectiveness criteria: Towards a competing values approach to organisational analysis'. *Management Science* 29(3), 363–377.

Quinn, R.E. (1988) *Beyond Rational Management: Mastering the Paradoxes and Competing Demands of High Performance.* San Francisco: Jossey-Bass.

Core quadrants

- **Why use it?** Core quadrants have proved to be very helpful in increasing mutual understanding and respect amongst people with opposing core qualities.

- **What does it do?** The core quadrants model of Ofman (2001) can help you to determine, describe and diagnose your core 'quality'.

- **When to use it?** The core quadrants can be used to find out what your strengths and weaknesses are, as well your 'pitfalls', 'challenges' and 'allergies'. Once you are aware of these, you can more easily recognise these characteristics in others as well. Furthermore, it gives you a better understanding of your reactions to others.

- **What questions will it help you answer?** What is my major pitfall (too much of your core quality), what is my biggest challenge (the opposite of your pitfall) and what is my allergy in terms of core qualities in others (the opposite of your core quality – and too much of a challenge)?

The big picture

Every person has certain core qualities that truly describe the 'self'. A core quality pervades every aspect of an individual's life, such as words, feelings, deeds and values. Stripped of all the conscious and unconscious external protective and regulatory barriers of everyday life, your core quality describes 'the real you'. What is your core quality? The core quadrants model of Ofman (2001) can help you to determine, describe and diagnose your core quality (Figure 23.1).

When to use it

The core quadrants can be used to find out what your strengths and weaknesses are, as well as your pitfalls, challenges and allergies. Once you are aware of these, you can more easily recognise these characteristics in others as well. Furthermore, it gives you a

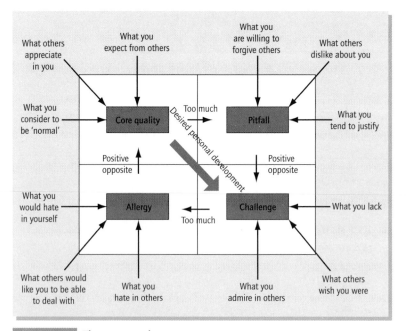

Figure 23.1 The core quadrants Source: based on Ofman (2001)

better understanding of your reactions to others. When you have a better understanding of your own core competencies, you can gain a greater insight into the rational problems of others, as well as increased self-awareness.

How to use it

Although it is difficult to put your finger precisely on your core quality, it is easier when you look at it from different perspectives:

■ What is your major *pitfall*? (Too much of your core quality.)

■ What is your biggest *challenge*? (The opposite of your pitfall.)

■ What is your *allergy* in terms of core qualities in others? (The opposite of your core quality – and too much of a challenge.)

The core quadrant shows the different, yet interdependent, perspectives of your core quality. An understanding of, and active consideration for, these core qualities, pitfalls, challenges and allergies strongly increases efficiency and effectiveness of human interaction.

The power of this model lies in the fact that it offers four perspectives on a 'core quality'. Nevertheless, there are subtle differences. The same core quality may have slightly different pitfalls, challenges and allergies. It is therefore important to specify the quadrants in more detail for each individual.

To this end, Ofman suggests that three additional perspectives be added to each of the four elements, which can then be combined to form a personalised 'super quadrant':

■ something that *you* would say, feel, like, condone, wish, miss or hate *about yourself*;

■ something that *you* would say, feel, like, condone, wish, miss or hate *about others*;

■ something that *others* would say, feel, like, condone, wish, miss or hate *about you*.

The super quadrant is uncomfortably revealing: inconsistencies between the three 'super quadrant' perspectives are a relatively sure indicator that you are not who and/or how you want to be. You are, in fact, trying to hide your true feelings, avoid your pitfalls and curb your dislike of your allergy. In other words, you are 'acting'.

Incongruity in a core quadrant can also be an indicator that you might be describing the symptoms or effects of a pitfall. For example, the core quality 'enthusiasm' could lead to the pitfall fanaticism, leading to negative feedback, causing disappointment, fuelling retreat and, eventually, egotism. Yet, egotism itself is not the pitfall.

The core quadrants can be used to prepare for meetings where people with opposing core qualities interact. Instead of a confrontation, both parties can muster (more) respect and try to learn from each other.

The final analysis

Core quadrants have proved to be very helpful in increasing mutual understanding and respect amongst people with opposing core qualities. There is, however, an inherent danger in 'classifying' oneself or someone else incorrectly. It is important to involve others in the perspectives.

At the end of the day, the continual effort of remaining aware of one's core quality, though difficult, is perhaps the closest approximation of being true to oneself and succeeding in life.

Reference

Ofman, D.D. (2001) *Inspiration and Quality in Organizations*, 12th edn. Antwerp: Kosmos-Z&K.

24

Cultural dimensions (Hofstede)

- **Why use it?** Hofstede's cultural dimensions can be used to develop an effective strategy to cooperate with people from various countries and cultural backgrounds.

- **What does it do?** Hofstede's cultural dimensions model can be useful in creating awareness of the various cultural differences that become apparent when an organisation starts to operate internationally.

- **When to use it?** Hofstede's cultural dimensions model can help to avoid cultural misunderstandings and communication failures, helping organisations get off to a good start with potential clients or partners.

- **What question will it help you answer?** How can I become more effective when interacting with people from other cultures?

The big picture

Hofstede's cultural dimensions can be used to develop an effective strategy to cooperate with people from various countries. By studying survey data on the values of employees at IBM in over 50 countries, Hofstede concluded that there were big differences in these cultural values. In many countries, the challenges and problems around these cultural values seemed the same, but the interpretations and subsequent solutions differed strongly by country. His model is an aid to becoming more effective when interacting with people from other countries. The types of (different) values identified in the study represent the four dimensions of culture:

1 Power distance

2 Individualism/collectivism

3 Masculinity/femininity

4 Uncertainty avoidance.

However, based on the differences between western and eastern countries, a fifth dimension was added, namely:

5 Long-term orientation.

Knowing the differences between national cultures makes it possible to understand specific behaviour. Becoming aware of and recognising these differences is the first step to becoming more effective when interacting in multicultural environments (Figure 24.1).

When to use it

The chances are that most of us have business dealings with people from different cultural backgrounds on a daily basis. Internationalisation leads to more international clients, partners and suppliers, and may also result in hiring employees from all

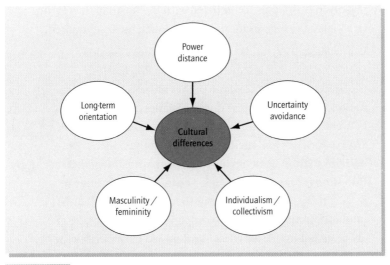

Figure 24.1 Hofstede's dimensions of culture

Source: after Hofstede, Hofstede and Minkov (2010)

around the world. This trend increases the risk of cultural misunderstandings and failures. Hofstede's cultural dimensions model and the scores of nationalities involved on these dimensions may help to prevent these frictions and to get off to a good start with potential clients or partners.

How to use it

Hofstede's cultural dimensions model is not a guideline for interaction between people; it merely helps to understand certain behaviour:

▦ **Power distance index (PDI)** is the extent to which the less powerful members of organisations and institutions accept and expect power to be distributed unequally amongst individuals. If an Austrian and a Malaysian marketing manager working on the same hierarchical level within an organisation are compared, the difference in PDI becomes visible. The Malaysian manager (high PDI) has hardly any responsibility or power compared with the Austrian (low PDI). In a Malaysian organisation, power is much more centralised.

■ **Individualism (IDV)** (and collectivism, on the other side of the continuum) describes the relationship between the individual and the collective that prevails in a given nation. Individualism pertains to societies in which the ties between individuals are loose; everyone is expected to look after themselves and their immediate family. Collectivism pertains to those societies in which people are integrated into strong, cohesive in-groups. The in-groups continue to protect these people throughout their lifetime in exchange for unquestioning loyalty. In US companies, for instance, people are more self-interested and less interested in the well-being of the whole team than is the case in Asian companies.

■ **Masculinity (MAS)** is the opposite of femininity. These constructs refer to the differences between the sexes. In masculine cultures, assertiveness is the predominant characteristic, as opposed to personal goals and nurturing. In Japan, ambition, competitiveness and accumulation of wealth and material possessions are valued, whereas in Sweden relationships and quality of life are much more important.

■ **Uncertainty avoidance index (UAI)** indicates to what extent a culture programmes its members to feel threatened by ambiguous situations. Uncertainty-avoiding cultures try to minimise the possibility of such situations by strict laws and rules and safety and security measures. In addition, these cultures are characterised by long-term employment. Others have a low UAI and are therefore more likely and relatively willing to take risks.

■ **Long-term orientation (LTO)** vs short-term orientation. Values associated with long-term orientation are thrift and perseverance; values associated with short-term orientation are respect for tradition, fulfilling social obligations and protecting one's 'face'. Asian countries, such as China,

Vietnam and Japan, score relatively high on the LTO index, whilst western countries, such as Australia, Germany and Norway, score relatively low.

Do's

◾ Realise that the actions and reactions of people from other countries may be completely different to what you are used to.

Don'ts

◾ Be aware that the possible differences are no guarantee for effective interaction, as no two individuals are alike.

The final analysis

Hofstede's cultural dimensions model has been useful in creating awareness of the various cultural differences that become apparent when a firm starts to operate internationally. However, during the past few decades, distances have decreased, cultures have mingled and differences are often less visible. In addition, one could question the ratings of some countries, depending on whether all cultural groups within that country are represented or not. In either case, ratings on dimensions may vary amongst the inhabitants of that specific country. Finally, no two individuals are alike, and one must therefore realise that misunderstandings can still happen.

References

Hofstede, G., Hofstede, G.J. and Minkov, M. (2010) *Cultures and Organizations: Software of the Mind*, 3rd revised edn. London: McGraw-Hill.

Hofstede, G. (2001) *Culture's Consequences: Comparing Values, Behaviours, Institutions, and Organisations across Nations*. Thousand Oaks CA: Sage Publications.

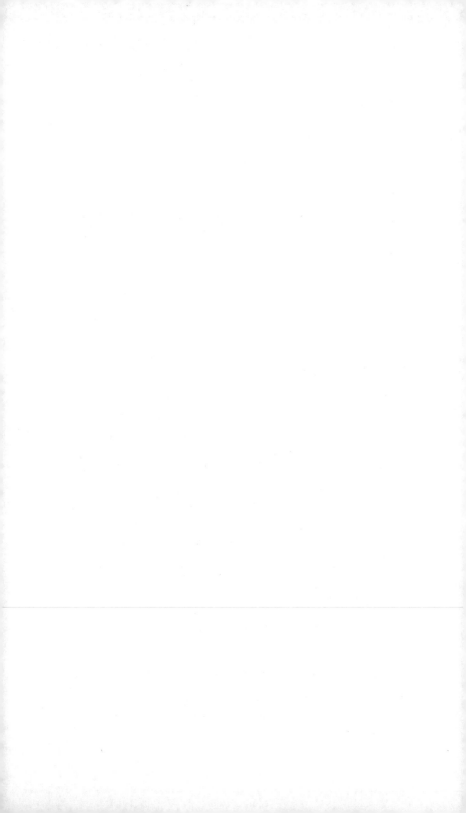

Seven habits of highly effective people (Covey)

- **Why use it?** Covey claims that highly effective people have seven habits that make them very successful in life and business, and he argues that highly effective managers do exactly what they feel is both right and important, and they do it consciously.

- **What does it do?** The model provides a self-help programme based on an inside-out approach.

- **When to use it?** This model is useful to gain an insight into what makes people successful and effective. It is also useful as a model for self-help to improve your individual performance and effectiveness.

- **What question will it help you answer?** What drives people to do the things they do and how can they become effective in doing them?

The big picture

Wildly popular throughout the 1990s and into the twenty-first century, Stephen Covey (1989) has changed the face of many an ambitious manager's bedside table. Covey claims that highly effective people have *seven habits* that make them very successful in life and business (see Figure 25.1):

1 Be proactive.

2 Begin with the end in mind.

3 Put first things first.

4 Think win–win.

5 First understand, and then be understood.

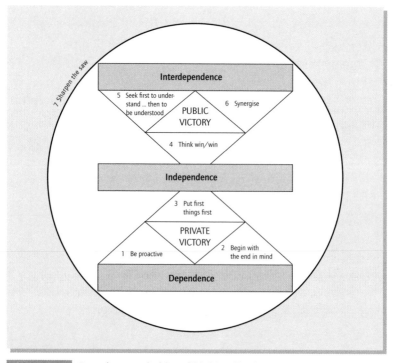

Figure 25.1 Covey's seven habits of highly effective people

Source: after Covey (1989)

6 Synergise.

7 'Sharpen the saw'.

In addition, Covey argues that highly effective managers do exactly what they feel is both right and important, and they do it consciously.

When to use it

The seven habits model is a theory that tries to give an insight into why successful people are successful, in both business and in their personal lives. It is therefore highly applicable for leaders and managers. The model provides a self-help programme, based on an inside-out approach. According to Covey, our personal paradigms affect our interactions with others, which in turn affect how others interact with us. Improving interactions thus starts with a thorough understanding of our own paradigms and motives. To become successful, one should examine how effectively one acts and interacts.

How to use it

According to Covey, one first has to break loose from being dependent on others. People may become independent by adopting the first three habits:

- **Be proactive.** From now on, *you* take responsibility for your own behaviour. You don't blame circumstances, conditions, or – perhaps most importantly – your conditioning for your behaviour. You actively choose your response to any situation and any person. You must be prepared to respond in a way that makes you feel proud. If that requires extra hard work or makes you feel uncomfortable, so be it.

- **Begin with the end in mind.** Whatever you undertake, you must visualise the result or future that you want to achieve. You have a clear vision of where you want to go, or you will not go there at all. You know exactly what you want to accomplish, or you choose not to accomplish it at all. You live your life and make decisions according to your deeply held beliefs, principles or 'fundamental truths'.

- **Put first things first.** By taking full control and remaining disciplined, you can focus on the most important, but not necessarily the most urgent, activities. Covey's list of such important activities includes building relationships, writing a personal mission statement, making a long-range plan, doing your workout and preparing for that presentation next week. Do all those things now that otherwise would be squeezed in at the last minute, delayed or even dismissed. They will help you eliminate those urgent activities that recently topped your overweight to-do list, but really were not as important. Now that you have reached the point of being independent, and you are using your time to *pursue* your most important goals in life *effectively*, you must increase your effectiveness with others around you.

- **Think win–win.** You must believe in 'abundance' – there is plenty for everyone. One person's success does not necessarily require someone else's failure. You seek solutions to problems that allow all parties involved (including yourself) to benefit.

- **Understand first, before trying to be understood.** By this means you can make people around you feel like winners. You might actually learn something from them in the process, now that you have finally decided to shut up and listen. In fact, you must listen with the firm intention of understanding the other person fully and deeply on an intellectual, analytical and emotional level. Diagnose before you prescribe, says Covey.

- **Synergise.** Finally, you need to open your mind to fresh, creative ideas. You become an agent for innovation, a trailblazer and a pathfinder. You are convinced that the whole is greater than the sum of its parts. You value differences between people and try to build upon those differences (see references, and further reading on Belbin's team roles, Chapter 20). You think of creative ways to resolve conflict.

- **'Sharpen the saw'.** You have now reached a stage of interdependence. You are effective and admired by family, friends and co-workers. Nevertheless, you should never allow yourself to rest on your laurels. You must constantly trying to improve yourself, and retain a relentless eagerness to learn and explore.

The final analysis

The question is, what drives people to do the things they do, and how can they become happy doing them? Covey appeals to business managers and all other professionals who take themselves seriously, by bringing it all back to one commonly understood concept: effectiveness. What happened to that world trip you dreamed of 20 years ago? Effectiveness, and having the time to do all those important things that make us love life and make others love us, is the ultimate dream of the overworked manager.

References

Covey, S.R. (1989) *The Seven Habits of Highly Effective People.* New York: Simon & Schuster.

Covey, S.R. (2004) *The 8th Habit: From Effectiveness to Greatness.* New York: Free Press.

What did you think of this book?

We're really keen to hear from you about this book, so that we can make our publishing even better.

Please log on to the following website and leave us your feedback.

It will only take a few minutes and your thoughts are invaluable to us.

www.pearsoned.co.uk/bookfeedback

Ten useful books to read next

If you would like to get a more comprehensive list of management models, we recommend:

1 Van den Berg, G. and Pietersma, P. (2014) *Key Management Models: The 75+ Models Every Manager Needs to Know*, 3rd edn, FT Publishing.

   Management models – love them or hate them, they crop up all the time. Models provide a framework for improving business performance, so if you're a manager, or studying business, then it's really important you know what they are and how to use them. *Key Management Models* has the winning combination of brevity and clarity, so it is the essential guide to all the management models you'll ever need to know about. This book gives you short, practical overviews of the top classic and cutting-edge management models in an easy-to-use, ready-reference format. Whether you want to remind yourself about models you've already come across, or want to find new ones, you'll find yourself referring back to it again and again. And you'll wonder what you ever did without it!

2 Walsh, K. (2008) *Key Management Ratios*, 4th edn, Pearson.

   Key Management Ratios is an antidote to any fear of finance. Drawing data from 200 companies worldwide, the book brings clarity and simplicity to its explanation of every measure and shows how they all link together to drive your business. From cash flow and profit to ROI and ROTA, its unique approach remains as classic as ever, bringing a simple and visual understanding to a complex subject.

3 Evans, V. (2013) *Key Strategy Tools: The 80+ Tools for Every Manager to Build a Winning Strategy*, Pearson.

Covering 88 tools and framed within an innovative strategy development process, the Strategy Pyramid, this user-friendly manual takes you through each step of the process. Whether analysing your market, building competitive advantage or addressing risk and opportunity, you'll find the strategic thinking tools you need at every stage in your strategy development. Let *Key Strategy Tools* be your guide to developing a winning strategy for your firm. Cherry-pick the most useful approaches for your business and create a robust strategy that withstands investor scrutiny and becomes your roadmap to success.

4 Strong, H. (2014) *Marketing and Management Models: A Guide to Understanding and Using Business Models,* Business Expert Press.

Modern business practice, especially in the field of marketing, depends on the integration of creative and analytical thinking. One of the tools in this process is the use of management models to guide business decisions. However, the inherent power of the models is only released when the people applying them have the ability to gather relevant information and interpret the relationships between the variables in the model. This book examines the role of some of the most popular management models and will help you determine when they should be applied. In addition, it suggests which models may be relevant and, more importantly, identifies the type of information needed to implement them; and also reduces the complexity of these models through a logical and systematic approach.

5 Newton, R. (2011) *The Management Book*, Financial Times Prentice Hall.

The Management Book picks out the top issues you are likely to face on a daily basis as a manager. It shows you how to maximise your own performance and that of your team in each of these areas so that you deliver the outstanding results you want. Clearly structured in 36 short sections, this practical book provides rapid, accessible advice on all the essential management challenges. Focusing on the manager's key role – managing teams to get things done – this book looks at the essential parts of management from unusual perspectives and different angles.

6   McKeown, M. (2012) *The Strategy Book*, Pearson.

Thinking strategically is what separates managers and leaders. This book teaches you the fundamentals about how to create a winning strategy and lead your team to deliver it. From understanding what strategy can do for you, through to creating a strategy and engaging others with strategy, this book offers practical guidance and expert tips. It is peppered with punchy, memorable examples from real leaders winning (and losing) with real-world strategies.

7   Burtonshaw-Gunn, S. (2008) *The Essential Management Toolbox: Tools, Models and Notes for Managers and Consultants*, John Wiley.

A must have for all practising and aspiring consultants and strategists, this book covers a wide range of consultancy tools and techniques that are well displayed, well described and well referenced. The tools and techniques are helpfully divided into 20 recognisable skills sectors within management consultancy fields and specialisms. The depiction of the content with diagrams aids the process of quick reference and ease of understanding.

8   www.12manage.com, Jaap de Jonge (since 2006).

12manage is a knowledge network for managers, specialists and academics about management. Part of its services are an extensive management dictionary with more than 1000 management terms and an encyclopedia of hundreds of management methods, models and theories available in multiple languages, as well as an interactive user forum on contemporary management topics and issues.

9 **www.mindtools.com,** James Manktelow (since 1996).

Mindtools is an online platform that provides leadership, team management, problem-solving, decision-making, project management, personal productivity, team-working and communication skills that one needs to become an effective leader, great manager and successful in one's career. Mindtools offers online leadership, management and career development resources to busy professionals around the world, including an online repository with more than 900 skills, techniques, and tools explained in detail, hundreds of expert interviews and online articles and books, and numerous online (cloud-based) training courses.

10 Van den Berg, G. and Pietersma, P. (2013) *Eight Steps to Strategic Success*, Kogan Page.

Eight Steps to Strategic Success brings together the most well-known and most powerful strategy models, from Porter's five forces to the balanced scorecard. It presents a clear, empirically proven eight-step method for formulating strategy that works in practice, not just in theory. For each step, the book describes the key parts of the process, how to avoid the potential pitfalls, and points to the most useful strategic models and frameworks. Readers can see the process in action by following the intriguing case study that unfolds throughout the book. One of the critical determinants of strategic success is to see strategy not just as a planning exercise but also as a process that involves dialogues with multiple stakeholders, both internal and external to your organisation. This concept of dialogue is integrated into every phase of the eight-step approach and is at the heart of its effectiveness in creating a results-focused strategy that delivers in practice.

Glossary of terms

Benchmarking A systematic and structured approach to comparing your company's performance and processes to other companies and best practices.

Business model Description of the rationale of how an organisation creates and captures value and delivers it to its customers, its employees and itself in both economic, social, cultural and other contexts.

Business strategy Stating the goals and targets for the organisation or parts of the organisation and the way the organisation intends to achieve those. Often related to answering the question 'How shall we compete in the business we are in?'.

Change management An approach to transitioning an organisation or parts of the organisation, including all the individuals working in it, to a desired future state. Often it is often strongly associated with changes in culture, attitude or behaviour.

(Corporate) governance The structure and processes by which an organisation is controlled and directed, including the distribution of rights and responsibilities among different participants in this structure and including the rules and procedures for taking decisions about the organisation's future. Good corporate governance adheres to universally accepted principles of how to let the corporate governance function with the best intentions for the organisation.

Corporate strategy Stating the overall aim and direction (objectives) for the organisation as a whole. Often related to answering the question 'What business should we be in?'.

Cost accounting (direct and indirect costs) A field in management that relates to the provision of detailed information on all costs and the cost efficiency of the organisation in order to control current activities of the organisation and to assess and evaluate optimisation plans and alternative activities for the future.

Discounted Cash Flow (DCF) A method for valuing and appraising investments, based on the total cash flow an investment will generate in the future. Future cash flows are discounted to their present day values taking the time value of money into consideration.

Economic value added (EVA) A measure of higher-than-expected return on capital employed: the profit earned minus the cost of financing the activities that led to that profit.

Finance A field in management that relates to the allocation of assets and liabilities, and the effective and efficient management of them in such a manner as to accommodate the organisation in reaching its objectives.

Human resource management (HR; HRM) A field in management that relates to the maximisation of employee performance in order to enable the organisation to reach its objectives. It includes facilitating the organisation in managing the workforce, with activities such as recruitment, performance appraisal and rewarding, training and development.

Innovation The development and bringing to the market of something new, original and important in its field that (potentially) will bring the market (or society) to the next level.

Kaizen Means 'good change' in Japanese. It is a method for continually improving all functions in the organisation and involves all employees.

Leadership The ability to guide or lead a group of people or an organisation to pursue a common objective.

Lean (management) A production philosophy that considers the expenditure of resources in any aspect other than the direct creation of value for the customer to be wasteful, and thus a target for elimination.

Management model A tool, approach or technique to support management in making decisions, setting objectives, aligning activities to objectives, and coordinating efforts and people within the organisation. Often based on theory and accompanied with a graphical representation of some sort, like a matrix, schedule or diagram.

Marketing A field in management that relates to all communication with potential and current customers, in terms of both their wishes and demands and the organisation's offering of products and services. It includes looking for and choosing target markets, and communicating the attractiveness and value of the organisation's offerings to the markets the organisation had chosen and is active in.

Net present value (NPV) The resulting value when all future in-going and outgoing cash flows are discounted to their present day values including any (upfront) investment. See also DCF.

Operations A field in management that relates to all activities involved in designing, optimising and controlling the process of production. It concerns both efficiency in the use of resources when converting input into outputs, and effectiveness to meet customer requirements and organisational objectives.

Organisational culture The collectively shared mental assumptions within an organisation – of (subgroups of the) people working in that organisation – that guide interpretation and action of all working in the organisation. These shared assumptions define appropriate behaviour for various situations and is taught to new organisational members as the right way of perceiving, thinking and feeling.

Product/market combinations (PMC) The breakdown of the organisation's offering of products and services into both specific product (and services) groups and specific markets or customer groups. When this breakdown is plotted in a matrix, with the specific products (services) on one axis and the specific markets (customer groups) on the other axis, different combinations can be found: the so-called product/market combinations.

Sales A field in management that relates to all commercial activities of the organisation that are aimed at selling its products and services for the highest reward.

Six sigma A set of techniques, tools and statistical methods for improving the quality of process outputs by identifying and removing the causes of defects and by minimising variety in the process. Employees improving process with six sigma methods are often trained in its techniques and tools and can be recognised by their 'coloured belts' (black, brown, green, yellow, etc.).

Stakeholder A non-shareholding person or other organisation that has a stake in the success of the organisation, for instance employees, customers, suppliers, trade unions, governments and local communities.

Supply chain A chain of organisations, each with their own specific activities, that transforms natural resources into a product or service for consumers. Often a supply chain consists of multiple organisations in multiple countries in multiple industries. In sophisticated supply chains products can be re-entered at a certain point in the supply chain (recycling).

SWOT analysis or TOWS analysis A structured method to evaluate and assess the organisation's abilities in terms of strengths (S) and weakness (W) and the possibilities the organisation has in its market in terms of opportunities (O) and threats (T).

Value chain The chain of key primary and supporting activities of the organisation to deliver its products and services.

Index